Star Sets

Drum Kits Of The Great Drummers • By Jon Cohan

Foreword by Bill Bruford

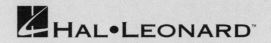

HAL•LEONARD™

Star Sets

Drum Kits Of The Great Drummers • By Jon Cohan

Foreword by Bill Bruford

Front Cover Photos (clockwise from upper left):

Buddy Rich	Frank Driggs Collection
John Bonham	Jeffrey Mayer/Star File
Ginger Baker	Jeffrey Mayer/Star File
Chick Webb	Frank Driggs Collection
Keith Moon	Star File
Grateful Dead	Jon Cohan

ISBN 0-7935-3489-5

HAL•LEONARD™
CORPORATION
7777 W. BLUEMOUND RD. P.O. BOX 13819 MILWAUKEE, WI 53213

TABLE OF CONTENTS

1960s THE NEW FRONTIER

1970s... THE BEAT GOES ON

Every effort was made to insure the accuracy of the diagrams and information in this book. Drummers sometimes change the arrangement of their kits as often as every day. Just because Sid Catlett played a Ludwig & Ludwig kit with two tom-toms on Friday doesn't mean he did the same thing on Saturday. The diagrams are intended to reflect a certain period in the drummer's career.

It is not a judgement on the quality or importance of a drummers work if a drummer was not included in this book. The drummers I selected were chosen to illustrate a wide variety of styles and drum kits. I would hope to include many more great drummers if I have the opportunity to write a second volume...

Please send any inquiries or comments to:

Jon Cohan
Drum Heaven
P.O. Box 1831
Jamaica Plain, MA. 02130

The photographs in this book were scanned on the Kodak Photo CD Imaging Workstation. Special Thanks to Steve Morse, David Semperger, Danielle Pucci, Bill and Carol Smith, and all the wonderful staff at Boston Photo Imaging.

AUTHOR'S NOTES AND ACKNOWLEDGEMENTS

Without the great help and encouragement of the people listed on this page, this book would have never seen the light of day. My sincere thanks go out to every one who assisted in making the dream come true.

My daughter, Leila Cohan, for the title and inspiration

Leon and Heidi Cohan for their understanding support

Annamarie Greco for her love and encouragement

Mark and Cindy Lammie of LslashLdesign for their incomparable design talents

Brad Smith, Chris Albano, Pete Schultz, and Sue Gedemer at Hal Leonard Corporation

Bill Bruford

John DeChristopher, Lennie DiMuzio, Colin Schofield, and John King at Zildjian

Derek Wiseman at Pearl

Todd Trent at Ludwig

Rick Van Horn and Modern Drummer magazine

Tim Cohan for his command of the English language

Fabian Jolivet, photo agent and drummer extraordinaire

Manny Wise

Scotty Doucette

Harry Cangany

Jim Pettit

Terry Cryer for his wonderful photographs

John Aldridge for his help and his tireless dedication to vintage drums

Chet Falzerano

Chad Smith in the house!

Andy Doerschuck at DRUM!

Airto Moreira and Flora Purim

Andy Florio

Esther Smith at Rutgers

John Good at Drum Workshop

Paul Beauchemin

Rob Cook

Joe Hibbs at Tama

Dennis McNally, Bill Grillo, Ramrod and the Grateful Dead

Hal Blaine for his assistance and inspiration

Joe MacSweeny of Eames Drum Co. for keeping the art of drum making alive

Ian Dickson

Tim Motion

Jim Robison

Jeffrey Mayer

Bob Henrit

Dave Abbruzzese

John Sheridan for Beatles info

Alan Slutsky for Motown info

Larry Bunker

Rich King

FOREWORD BY BILL BRUFORD

Even before the music begins, you can tell so much about the drummer by having a close look at his kit. There are hundreds of percussion instruments in the world, and the man to whom you are about to listen has brought along just these, and only these. Why? Will he be approaching the music in the manner of a European classical percussionist who, like a surgeon about to operate, will select, from many, the right tools for the job? Or has he brought half a dozen instruments secure in the knowledge that he has all he needs to generate the whispers, roars, snarls, tension, and release that will be his pleasure that evening? Is his kit full of small, unusual, and highly personal sounds, whose timbre identifies him immediately (Airto Moreira), or will he perform on the neutral "Steinway" of drum kits (kick, snare, and tom-toms) and let us identify him by style, touch, and tuning (Max Roach, Elvin Jones)?

So many choices, options, and decisions have been made and taken before a note is played, and for a drummer these options manifest themselves in his choice of tackle. From the Vaudeville/Calliope look of Chick Webb, through the kick-snare-and-tom-toms look of the classic jazz, to today's huge high-power, big drum leviathans of stadium metal, and the electronic or electro-acoustic sets of today's modernists, the design and components of the kit speak volumes about what you are about to hear, and how fast, slow, quietly, or loudly you're going to hear it.

What you are about to read is an exhaustive run-down of who played what, when, and why. The ever-changing sound of the drummer, from the turn of the century to the turn of the millennium, hasn't happened by accident, hasn't necessarily happened smoothly, and it definitely hasn't finished happening. As the drummer embarks on his lifetime manipulation of pulse and metre, rhythm and timbre, he also enters upon a parallel search for the perfect kit upon which to manipulate. Jon Cohan has provided us with a splendid pictorial essay of the results.

Bill Bruford

Surrey, England

Summer 1994

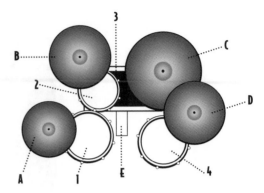

Jon Cohan's Kit 1994...Various drums w/Various cymbals

1... 6½ x 14" Drum Heaven Galaxy Custom
     Snare Drum
2... 8 x 12" Eames 12-Ply Tom-Tom
3... 22" 1957 Slingerland Red Sparkle
     Bass Drum
4... 14 x 14" WFL Red Sparkle Floor Tom or
     15 x 15" Eames 12-Ply Floor Tom

A... 14" Hi-hats, Paiste 2000 Top,
     Zildjian K Heavy Bottom
B... 16" Avedis Zildjian 1960s Paper Thin
     Crash
C... 20" Zildjian Medium Ride
D... 16" Paiste 2000 or Istanbul K. Zildjian
E... DW 5000 Bass Drum Pedal

INTRODUCTION BY JON COHAN

I've never considered myself an "equipment nerd" (although you don't write a book about drum sets unless you have at least a passing obsession with lugs, strainers, and tension rods), but I have always been infatuated with the sound of the kit. I remember as a kid growing up in Michigan, being transfixed with the drumming on my brother's James Brown, Who, and Fifth Dimension records. There was something in the grooves of those 45s that seemed so urgent and exciting. I still recall exactly where I was the first time I heard Bernard Purdie's classic take on Aretha Franklin's "Rock Steady" on a hand-held transistor radio. I always viewed drummers as the thankless heroes of music, supplying the feel and pulse that made all the feet tap and heads bob.

My first drum set was a used sparkling pink champagne Slingerland affair with matching snare and Gene Krupa instructional booklet. I loved messing around with that kit, sanding and refinishing the inside of the shells, cleaning the hardware, and putting different contact papers on it to change its appearance. The hobby turned into a love affair culminating in the forming of my own company, Drum Heaven, as an outlet for my passion. I sold and restored vintage drums before designing and building the Galaxy custom snare drum.

At first, some of the drummers I interviewed found it odd that anyone would write an entire book on equipment. Many were reluctant to talk about their kits, reminding me that it's not the drums but the drummer that makes the music sound good. The more we talked, the more we discovered that everyone has had

a favorite snare drum or special cymbal that they get starry-eyed about. Your sound and style define you as a musician. Your choice of equipment is as much a reflection of your personality as your playing. Drummers are often identified with their drums; think of Gene Krupa and his Radio Kings, Ringo Starr and his Oyster Black Ludwigs, and Elvin Jones and his Gretsch drums. These drummers all had styles that were closely intertwined with the instruments they played.

I found out while writing this book that not much has really changed since the drum set evolved out of the vaudeville pits and riverboat decks where it was born. There is not that wide a gulf between Chick Webb's and Bill Bruford's drum kits. Sure, we have triple-braced cymbal stands and electronic trigger pads, but the essence of what the drum set's job is has not changed. Rhythm is there to illuminate, accent, and enliven music. The drummer and his instrument are there to fulfill that promise.

What follows on these pages would not have been possible without the love, inspiration, and support I received from my daughter Leila Cohan and my partner Annamarie Greco, or the guidance and encouragement of Brad Smith, the greatest friend and adviser a drummer could ever hope for. It is to them that I dedicate this book.

The Beat Goes On...
Jon Cohan
October 1994

THE NEW
"NITE CLUB"
OUTFIT
No. 5325

$350.00

WITH LEEDY "AUTOGRAPHS
OF THE STARS" PYRALIN AND
NICKEL METAL PARTS

The new Nite Club Outfit is distinctively different in appearance, drumistically correct in every detail and complete in makeup. Finished in the exclusive new Leedy "Autographs of the Stars" pyralin—top-time Leedy drummers' authentic autographs indelibly and permanently processed in a star-studded blue background—this outfit packs

THE "NITE CLUB" OUTFIT
In Leedy "Autographs of the Stars" Pyralin and Nickel Metal Parts

1—No. 780 8"x14" Broadway Parallel Swingster Snare Drum	$ 59.00
1—No. 5101 14"x28" Broadway Separate Tension Bass Drum	81.50
1—No. 8018 14"x16" Separate Tension Tunable Tom-Tom	47.00
1—No. 8036 15"x14" Separate Tension Tunable Tom-Tom	42.00
1—No. 8038 9"x13" Separate Tension Tunable Tom-Tom	33.00
1—No. 7010 "X-L" Pedal	10.00
1—No. 8800 New Leedy Arch Trap Rail attached to Bass Drum	5.75
1—No. 7118 Pair Bass Drum Wheel Spurs	5.00
1—No. 7255 Standard (Heavy) Snare Drum Stand	5.00
1—No. 7871 Bass Drum Tone Control	1.75
2—No. 9026 Heavy Duty Ratchet Tom-Tom Holders at $4.25 each	8.50
1—No. 7753 Set Tunable Tom-Tom Legs (Brackets bolted to 14"x16" Tom-Tom)	3.00
2—No. 9045 Heavy Duty Angle Extension Cymbal Holders at $1.50 each	3.00
1—No. 9042 15½" Arm Heavy Duty Non-Swing Cymbal Holder	1.75
1—9040 22½" Arm Heavy Duty Non-Swing Cymbal Holder	2.00
1—No. 7300 10" Stanople Cymbal—Thin	4.50
1—No. 7311 11" Zenjian Cymbal	8.00
1—No. 7312 12" Zenjian Cymbal	9.50
1—No. 7363 15" Chinese Sneeze Cymbal	6.00
1—No. 7563 Leedy High Boy Sock Cymbal Pedal	10.00
2—No. 7311 11" Zenjian Cymbals for High-Boy Sock Cymbal Pedal at $8.00 each	16.00
1—No. 9022 Combination Cow Bell and Wood Block Holder	1.75
1—No. 7796 4¼" Cow Bell	1.00
1—No. 7797 5" Cow Bell	1.20
1—No. 7680 7" Chee Foo Chinese Wood Block	1.00
1—No. 1644 Pair Rubber Handle Wire Brushes	1.00
1—No. 25 Pair Swing Six	.60

(No Substitutions or Omissions)

TOTAL VALUE $368.80
SPECIAL PRICE 350.00

Leedy Autograph Kit, 1941

Sonny Mann

1920-1945 DIXIELAND & SWING

Jess Altmiller
Fox Theatre
Philadelphia, Pa.

Jess Altmiller

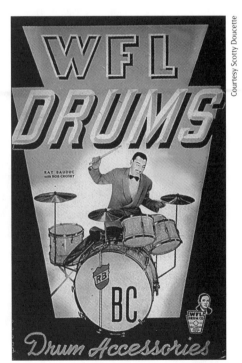

Ray Bauduc

Courtesy Harry Cangany

Assorted Leedy Stars

The drum set is one of New Orleans' greatest gifts to American popular music. When the brass parade bands stopped marching and settled down in the riverboats to play—when the dancers and comics in minstrel shows needed percussive accompaniment—when the blues came drifting off the plantations and mixed with Caribbean and African rhythms to make a new music called jazz, the drum kit was born.

In New Orleans near the turn of the century, musicians found much of their work in the cathouses, saloons, vaudeville pits and riverboats of that great delta city. The traditional brass band had to be pared down to fewer players to fit in these smaller spaces. Just one drummer was now faced with the task of recreating the sounds of many drummers. Military beats and rolls were modified to fit into the new ragtime music. By necessity, all the percussion instruments had to be gathered together and, in some way, played by one musician. This is how the traps evolved.

Courtesy Scotty Doucette

Barrett Deems

Courtesy Harry Cangany

Charlie Blake

Billy Gladstone

Ray McKinley

Frank Bird

Vaudeville Drummer

WFL Catalog

By the 1920s, vaudeville and jazz music reigned supreme, and drums were the bedrock of that revolution. As jazz bands came out of the brothels and into the ballrooms, the call was for a bigger sound to anchor the hefty brass and reed sections of the new groups. As a result, drum sets became more ornate and elaborate, and the drummer's role became that of a showman as well as a timekeeper.

The great swing bands came from Kansas City, Chicago, St. Louis, and New York. They traveled around the country, bringing their exciting music to the masses and creating new stars of many of the featured players. Drummers such as Sonny Greer, Gene Krupa, and Jo Jones became famous for their style and swing, while drum companies struggled to keep up with the heavy demand for product created by this new music.

This was the golden age of American drum making. Ludwig introduced the ornately engraved Black Beauty brass snare drum; Slingerland premiered its

Zutty Singleton

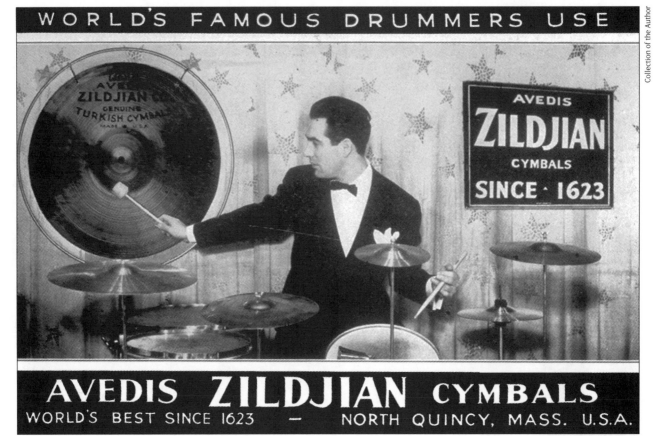

WORLD'S FAMOUS DRUMMERS USE

AVEDIS ZILDJIAN CYMBALS SINCE · 1623

AVEDIS ZILDJIAN CYMBALS
WORLD'S BEST SINCE 1623 — NORTH QUINCY, MASS. U.S.A.

Gene Krupa in early Zildjian Ad

Alberto Calderon

Jackie Cooper

Slingerland Artists

Rhythm Ben

Armand Zildjian, Jo Jones & Al Mercuri

famous Radio King solid maple shell; Leedy invented the floating drum head and self-aligning lug; and Gretsch originated the three-way tensioning system of the Gladstone snare drum. Hardware such as pedals, stands, and lugs became smartly designed both in form and function. All this was accomplished within a span of 15 years, some of it during the Great Depression. The craftsmanship of these drums still holds up to this day. Many of these vintage treasures are sought after and cherished not only as collector's items, but also as valid, useful instruments.

By far the most important advances during this era came from the drummers themselves. Giants like Baby Dodds, Zutty Singleton, and Chick Webb stand out as brave pioneers of the bandstand. They were the vanguards of a new frontier, creating a fresh vocabulary of rhythm that would forever change the way music was played and heard.

Gretsch Catalog Cover

Chauncey Morehouse

Andy Florio

Frankie Carlson

Mary McClanahan

Phil Rale

Massaging the calf in the 1950s.

If the history of modern drumming were to be viewed as a tree, with different branches representing swing, Bebop, blues, rock and roll, country, R&B, and Dixieland, then the roots of that tree would be proudly bear the name of Baby Dodds. Coming out of the New Orleans brass band tradition, Dodds translated that music from the drummer's customary marching setup to the drum kit. The artists he played with, such as his brother Johnny Dodds, Fate Marable, and Louis Armstrong, served as inspiration for the explosion of jazz that sprang up all over the country in the 1920s. Luckily, we have a wonderful journal of that era in Dodds' own words. *The Baby*

Baby Dodds, sans hi-hat, jams with Jimmy Noone and Roy Eldridge at the 3 Deuces, Chicago, in 1940.

Dodds Story (Louisiana State University Press, 1992) is a fascinating collection of drum set information, anecdotes, and drumming advice from the master's own mouth.

In 1918 Dodds was playing on the Mississippi riverboats with Louis Armstrong. "It was on the riverboats that I began using the rims instead of the woodblocks. The woodblock gave a loud sound, and I substituted the shell of the drums, and it sounded so soothing and soft.

"On the boat I also worked out the technique of hitting the cymbal with the sticks. I worked that out around 1919. Now everybody's using it, but it came from me on the riverboat. There was a side cymbal that used to be on the (bass) drum. I took that off and then it was a straight boom, boom, boom. Of course, I still used the two cymbals on top of the bass drum. There was a regular cymbal and a Chinese cymbal. The Chinese cymbal had a different tone." Drummer George Wettling also confirms that Dodds was the first drummer he heard who kept the famous broken triplet beat that became the standard pulse for ride cymbal playing.

"It was about the same time that I helped cause the sock (hi-hat) cymbals to be made. I was in St. Louis working on the steamboat and William Ludwig, the drum manufacturer, came on the boat for a ride. I used to stomp my left foot, long before other drummers did, and Ludwig asked me if I could stomp my toe instead of my heel. I told him 'I think so.' So he measured my foot on a piece of paper...two cymbals were set up and a foot pedal with them. One day he brought them along to try. It wasn't any good, so he brought another raised up about nine inches higher...I didn't like any part of them and I still don't. Some drummers can't drum without them. I can't drum with them."

Dodds also recorded an album of solos and stories for Folkways Records that provides excellent insight into his playing methods and attitudes towards the drums. "This drum jarred your insides," Dodds said of his bass drum. "This drum carried a 75-piece band. I tuned it accordingly to make it carry."

In the 1920s Dodds played a 28" Ludwig & Ludwig bass drum, four cowbells, a woodblock, a 10" Chinese tom-tom, a 6½" brass Ludwig Standard snare drum, a 14" or 16" Zildjian cymbal, and a 16" Chinese cymbal.

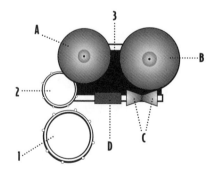

Baby Dodds' Kit Circa 1928...Ludwig & Ludwig drums w/Zildjian cymbals

1... 6½ x 14" white enamel Ludwig Standard Snare Drum
2... 10" tacked-head Chinese Tom-Tom
3... 14 x 28" white enamel Bass Drum
A... 14 or 16" "Jazz" Cymbal

B... 16" Chinese Crash Cymbal
C... 2-4 tuned Cowbells
D... Woodblock
Also assorted trap effects including: slapstick, whistle & ratchet

Zutty does some brush work on his Leedy Broadway Standard.

Mr. Singleton with Leedys at the St. Regis Hotel, New York City, 1938.

Zutty digs into his Leedys in Hempstead, N.Y., 1943.

Along with Baby Dodds, Zutty Singleton can be said to be the founding father of jazz drumming. Buddy Rich, Gene Krupa, Sid Catlett, Dave Tough, Jo Jones, and many others all tipped their hats to Zutty's spicy style of New Orleans playing. He had a loose, simple, funky approach to his instrument, always respecting and supporting the soloist he was accompanying and never getting in the way. He played drums behind some of the greats: Louis Armstrong, Jelly Roll Morton, Roy Eldridge, and Sidney Bechet.

Early in his playing days Zutty had the typical Dixieland setup of the type that evolved in New Orleans. He used a 5 x 14" Leedy Tudor snare drum, a big 28" bass drum with a tacked-head Chinese tom-tom attached to the rim, and various effects and cymbals.

Once Zutty became a Leedy endorser in the late thirties, he received a White Marine pearl-covered kit, which he played for at least 20 years. Even after the hi-hat (or Charleston Cymbals, as they were sometimes called) became popular in the thirties, most Dixieland drummers didn't use them, preferring to keep the syncopated pulse on the snare drum. Zutty would only use a hi-hat if the gig called for it. Otherwise he kept time on an 8"-deep Leedy Broadway Standard snare drum. Like Baby Dodds, Zutty kept his drums tuned to specific notes that coincided with the songs he was playing. His tom-toms, which varied in size from 11" to 14", were mounted on his bass drum, along with cowbells and a woodblock and other effects, which were essential to the New Orleans sound.

Zutty played a swinging quarter-note pattern on his bass drum, which was the basis and the heartbeat for New Orleans music. Drummer George Wettling, no slouch on the tubs himself, wrote of Singleton, "You can feel his beat even when you are sitting at the far end of the room. It seems as though it comes from his bass drum right up through the chair you are sitting in."

Television broadcast at CBS Studios.

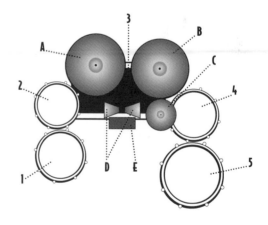

Zutty Singleton's Kit Circa 1941...Leedy drums, Marine Pearl

1... 8 x 14" Broadway Standard Snare Drum
2... 9 x 13 or 7 x 11" single-tension Tom-Tom
3... 28" Bass Drum
4... 12 x 14" single-tension bass-drum-mounted Tom-Tom
5... 14 x 16" Floor Tom

A... 16" Zildjian Cymbal
B... 15" riveted Chinese Crash
C... 6" Choke Cymbal
D... 2 Cowbells
E... Woodblock
Additional trap effects include: train whistle & ratchet.

Note: Zutty often would switch the 12 x 14" tom-tom to his left and put the 7 x 11" or 9 x 13" to his right. He might also omit the floor tom.

Chick in 1938, beaming behind his custom Gretsch-Gladstones.

In the 1930s, The Savoy Ballroom in Harlem was the mecca for any self-respecting drummer trying to hone his chops. Krupa, Rich, Tough, and many others all came to pay homage to the unlikely "King of the Savoy," Chick Webb.

The Savoy, or "The Track," as the hipsters called it, was the home of Chick Webb's band, and though many big bands challenged Webb to battle on the immense Savoy stage, none ever succeeded in stealing his crown. Basie, Duke, Goodman, and many others fell to the powerful swing of the Webb band, pushed ahead by its diminutive leader's playing.

Chick Webb was esteemed by so many drummers because of his uncanny ability to propel a band. Gene Krupa, who was just one of the many great drummers "cut" by Webb on the Savoy bandstand, wrote, "The man was dynamic; he could reach the most amazing heights...when he felt like it, he could cut down any of us."

Small in size, but huge in sound, Webb held court behind a dazzling custom-finished four-piece set of Gretsch-Gladstones. Each "White Oriental Pearl"-covered drum was inlaid with green sparkle baby chicks strolling around the circum-

The little king surveys his domain at the Savoy ballroom in 1937.

ference. Because of his small size, Chick had a special foot pedal extended so he could reach the bass drum with ease. Instead of metal rims, the Gladstone tom-toms had wood hoops inlaid with gold sparkle. Webb's cowbell, woodblock, temple blocks, Zildjian cymbals, and tom-tom were all attached to a rolling console that served double duty as an anchor for his 28" bass drum. He liked to use all these resources to create his surprising drum breaks, squeezing the most he could from his instruments. Listen to "Go Harlem" or "Squeeze Me" for examples of his crafty use of the entire kit. "If you never got a chance to hear that band live, you really missed something," Count Basie said in his autobiography. "Chick kept them all together with those drums."

Chick Webb, "King of Drums," adorns the cover of the 1939 Gretsch catalog.

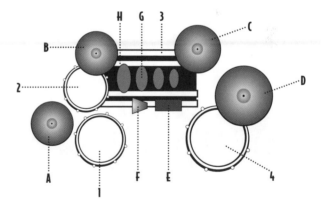

Chick Webb's Kit Circa 1938...Gretsch-Gladstone drums, White Oriental Pearl, w/Zildjian cymbals

1... 6½ x 14" Snare Drum		**C**... 13" Crash	
2... 9 x 13" Tom-Tom		**D**... 15" Chinese Swish	
3... 28" Bass Drum		**E**... Woodblock	
4... 14 x 16" Floor Tom		**F**... Cowbell	
A... 12" Hi-hats		**G**... 4 tuned Temple Blocks	
B... 12" Crash		**H**... Gretsch Wheeled Console	

Note: All drums and cymbals (except hi-hats) were attached to the Gretsch wheeled console. The cymbals were suspended from bent arms. Chick also had a special extension built so he could reach his foot pedals. The drums had custom inlaid sparkle designs.

Ace Drummer Man.

Gene in a 1940 publicity still.

It's a safe bet to say that Gene Krupa was the first bona fide superstar of the drum kit. "You couldn't help but notice Gene in those days," Louie Bellson said. "He brought drums to the foreground." Krupa's surefire combination of technical talent, inherent showmanship, and movie idol good looks caused his star to rise as high as any drummer who came before or after. His musical legacy can still be heard and seen in many of the drummers who followed the era that Krupa dominated. There are even bits of Gene's playing in the work of rock drummers like John Bonham, Keith Moon, and Carmine Appice.

What's often forgotten is that Gene Krupa made many contributions to the actual drum set itself. He was influential in developing the double-headed tunable tom-tom, as well as the Rapid strainer that was copied by all the drum companies of the day. His setup of a bass-drum-mounted 13" tom-tom and one or two floor toms became the standard configuration used by many players throughout popular music. "The 9 x 13" tom-tom became an institution because of Gene," says vintage-drum expert Andy Florio.

Gene Krupa's name is synonymous with Slingerland, but more importantly with Radio Kings. When Benny Goodman's band hit it big in the thirties, Krupa shot to fame as a featured player with his explosive playing and a fountain of rhythmic ideas. He became the anchor in Slingerland's growing endorser empire, eventually having a snare drum named after him. A 1941 Slingerland catalog claims, "There has been such a demand for this model, as well as other drums seen on these pages, that we have dedicated this model, in size 6½ x 14", to Krupa and it will be known exclusively as his particular design." Even today, one of the most prized vintage drums to be had by any collector is the Krupa model Radio King.

Krupa's crisp snare drum work was reminiscent of Zutty Singleton, Baby Dodds, and other New Orleans drummers he

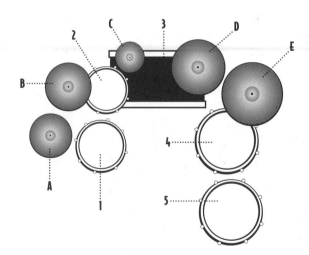

Gene Krupa's Kit Circa 1940s...Slingerland Radio King drums, Marine Pearl finish

1... 6½ x 14" Snare Drum   **A**... 12" Hi-hats

2... 9 x 13" Tom-Tom   **B**... 13" Crash Cymbal

3... 26" Bass Drum   **C**... 8" Splash Cymbal

4... 16 x 16" Floor Tom   **D**... 14" Cymbal

5... 16 or 18" Floor Tom   **E**... 16" Crash Cymbal

Note: Gene had custom cymbal stands with cast iron music stand feet for stability.

heard growing up in Chicago, and like those musicians he took great care in tuning his drums. He kept his snare drum tuned fairly high and favored a nice open sound on his tom-toms and bass drum. "Gene liked to stand out in the house before a show and have somebody play his drums so he could hear them from the audience's perspective," says Lennie DiMuzio of Zildjian.

Gene also loved to propel a band with cymbals, using his Zildjians to great effect when he kicked in a chorus. Although he changed cymbal sizes, he usually ended up with 12" hi-hats, a 7" or 8" splash, 13" and 16" medium thin crashes, and a 14" bass-drum-mounted ride cymbal. Later in his career, he switched to a larger ride cymbal, sometimes as big as 24".

All the elements of Gene's drums came together on songs like "Leave Us Leap," "Drum Boogie," and the infectious "Sing, Sing, Sing." One fact becomes clear after listening his work: if ever there was a guy in love with playing the skins, Gene Krupa would be that "drummin' man."

Gene swings London in the late 1950s.

The drum that launched a thousand dreams—
The 1941 Radio King.

The drummer as movie star—Krupa on the set in 1945.

Gene testing out the latest hi-hats at Zildjian in 1939.

Krupa exemplified the style of the swing era.

Gene Krupa, "King of Swing," 100% Slingerland Radio Kings.

Papa Jo and the tools of his trade.

Frank Driggs Collection

If you're looking up the definition of style in jazz drumming, look no further than Jo Jones. While some had more proficiency in other areas, no one could swing a tune like 'Papa' Jo. His playing with Count Basie in the thirties and forties still ranks as some of the greatest rhythm section work of all time. When the Basie band locked in, the time was so solid you could set your watch by it. Jones, along with Sid Catlett, helped close the gap between big band and bop drumming and change the drummer's role forever. His artful use of the hi-hat, brushes, innovative accents on the snare, and tastefully placed bass drum kicks influenced many drummers like Art Blakey and Kenny Clarke to step away from the traditional four-on-the-floor approach to jazz drumming and take the music in different directions.

But Jo was also a showman. He often kept a 16" floor tom on his left as well as his right side for the purpose of dramatic cross-hand sticking patterns. It was not unusual for him to play the set with his bare hands, or use his sticks on rims or stands to get the desired rhythmic and visual effect. His solos were always well crafted, smart, and entertaining.

Respected and admired by his peers for his sound and feel on the traps, Jones played in a loose, swinging fashion, kicking a band to life when the situation called for it. "You may think you're the boss," Count Basie once said about Jones, "but that drummer is really the head man."

Jones played Gretsch-Gladstones as well as Gretsch Broadkasters when he was with Basie. The drums, like the man himself, were always immaculate and perfectly in tune. Although he played big drums and cymbals, Jones had a remarkably light touch and rich sound. A Gretsch ad from the early forties proclaimed, "When Joe caresses his Gretsch-Gladstones the cash customers realize they're hearing the best drums in the world, handled by a lad who knows they give back all the feeling he puts into them." And feeling, it seems, was something Jo Jones had a surplus of.

Papa at a Basie recording session.

Framed by his Gretsch-Gladstone floor tom and Zildjian cymbal.

Taking some cymbals out for a spin at Zildjian.

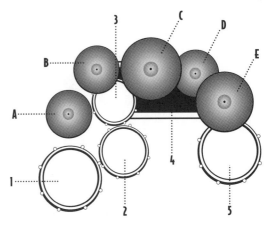

Jo Jones' Kit Circa 1940...Gretsch-Gladstone drums, White Oriental Pearl, w/Zildjian cymbals

1...	16 x 16" Floor Tom	A...	13" Hi-hat
2...	6½ x 14" Snare Drum	B...	13" Crash Cymbal
3...	9 x 13" Tom-Tom	C...	16" Cymbal
4...	26" Bass Drum	D...	13" Crash Cymbal
5...	16 x 16" Floor Tom	E...	15" Cymbal

Buddy and his Radio Kings in a 1941 publicity shot for the Tommy Dorsey Band.

"**B**est goddamn snare drum I ever played," Buddy Rich once said of his prized Slingerland Radio King, "The construction of that drum was perfect for the kind of drum sound that I'm looking for."

Although Buddy endorsed more drum companies than Liz Taylor had husbands, he remained faithful to Slingerland in the end. His final kit, which consisted of a vintage 1940s-era Radio King 5½" solid maple shell snare drum, a 26" bass drum, a 9 x 13" mounted tom, and two 16" floor toms, was assembled for him by Joe MacSweeney of Eames Drum Co.

"I gave Buddy the snare drum in April of 1983, right after his quadruple bypass operation,"says MacSweeney. "Joe Morello had told me that it would probably add a couple of years to Buddy's life to get an old Radio King again. Buddy dug the drum and said he'd love to find the rest of the set, so I went about putting it together. I gave it to him in August 1983. When I saw him later on that year, he had left Ludwig again and had the Radio Kings up on stage. I asked him if he liked the drums. He said, 'They're up there aren't they?' "

Along with the Radio Kings, Buddy used Ludwig Atlas hi-hat and cymbal stands as well as a Rogers bass drum pedal. His cymbals were Zildjian: a 6" splash, 14" hi -hats, 2-18" crash cymbals, thin and medium thin, and a ride cymbal alternating between 20 and 22".

Starting out in vaudeville as a child performer, Buddy grew into stardom with the Artie Shaw Band in the late 1930s. He became a Slingerland endorser during Krupa's reign of fame, but felt he would always play second seat to his friend Gene, so after World War II, he left Slingerland to be the star of WFL's stable.

"Buddy Traps," age 12, beats out a tattoo on a Super-Ludwig in this publicity still for a 1929 movie short.

A page from a 1950s WFL catalog.

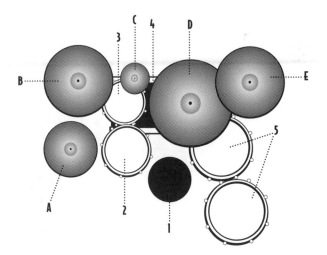

Buddy Rich's Kit Circa 1984...Slingerland Radio King drums, 1940s vintage White Marine Pearl, w/ Zildjian Cymbals, Ludwig Hi-hats & Cymbal Stands & Rogers Bass Drum Pedal

1... Canister Throne	**A**... 14" Hi-hats
2... 5½ x 14" Radio King Snare Drum	**B**... 18" Crash Cymbal Thin
3... 9 x 13" Tom-Tom	**C**... 6 or 8" Splash
4... 26" Bass Drum	**D**... 20 or 22" Ride
5... 2 16 x 16" Floor Toms	**E**... 18" Crash Cymbal Medium Thin

Note: Buddy sometimes used a 24" Swish Knocker.

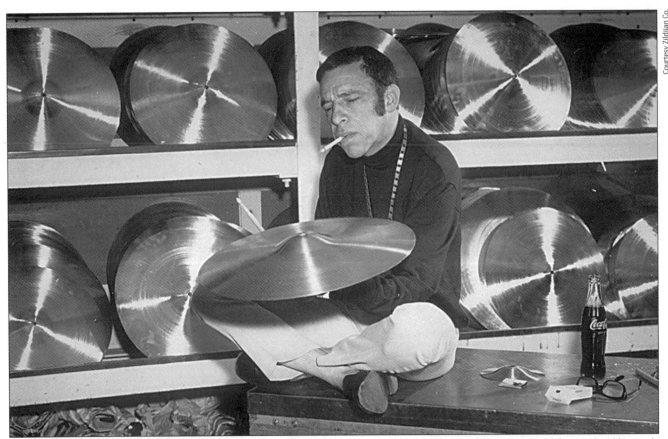

A cymbal undergoes the strenuous "Buddy" test in the Zildjian vault.

Buddy Rich

100% EQUIPPED WITH
SLINGERLAND DRUMS AND
AVEDIS ZILDJIAN CYMBALS

A Nehru-jacket-clad Rich gazes at his groovy new Slingerlands.

Bruce Allen

An older and wiser Buddy enjoying his vintage Radio Kings in 1985. Note the riveted "Swish Knocker" cymbal on the left.

Buddy also endorsed Ludwig, Rogers, Fibes, and Vox drums at different points in his long career. Along with Krupa and Ringo Starr, he was probably responsible for selling more kits than any other artist in history. His incredible technique and energy, along with his high visibility, made him the role model for thousands of drummers.

Besides having a personality as explosive as his playing, Buddy was also notoriously finicky when it came to his drums and cymbals. Mel Torme, in his wonderful biography of Rich, describes Buddy kicking a snare drum across the room in dissatisfaction. Although the drum might not have pleased the great one with its tone, most people would agree that Buddy Rich could have made a set of garbage cans sound fantastic.

Courtesy Zildjian Co.

Master Rich works his magic behind a Rogers kit.

Courtesy Zildjian Co.

A rare shot of Buddy playing Vox drums in the late 1960s.

Big Sid on stage for the Louie Armstrong band.

Ray Avery Archives

Big Sid Catlett was the 6'3" human bridge between two eras of jazz drumming, Swing and Bebop. Kenny Clarke, who is generally credited with being the father of Bop drumming, said simply, "We worshiped Big Sid."

Shelly Manne, another fine drummer, said of Catlett, "Big Sid and Klook (Kenny Clarke) were the first ones to move away from your accepted traditional way of playing by using more accents on the bass drum, more work on the ride cymbal, and things like that."

Despite his large frame, Catlett had a surprisingly soft touch on the skins, using his sense of dynamics and technique to make his statement within the framework of each tune. His fluid, responsive style earned him gigs with such great bandleaders as Benny Goodman, Louis Armstrong, Fletcher Henderson, and Dizzy Gillespie. "I loved Big Sid," said trumpeter Roy Eldridge. "He was so smooth. He had that weight without being noisy."

"His time was so sure, his taste so pure, and the way he took rhythmic charge was an inspiration to all the musicians," wrote jazz critic George T. Simon. "Big Sid was quite a giant."

Big Sid became a Ludwig endorser in the late 1930s, showing up behind a shiny four-piece Marine Pearl kit with Louis Armstrong's band. Like his idol Zutty Singleton, Big Sid preferred a 28" bass drum, beating out a pulse strong enough to swing anything from a big orchestra to a small Bop quartet. He liked to use his many cymbals to play unorthodox ride patterns and punctuate his bass drum accents. A Ludwig ad from 1939 states, "The 'Solid Cinder' is the hottest drummer in town. Sid Catlett, with a style of his own cooking, swings 'em hot on Ludwig drums."

The "Solid Cinder" caught in mid stroke at a 1940s rehearsal.

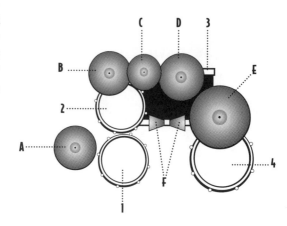

Sid Catlett's Kit Circa 1941...Ludwig & Ludwig drums, White Avalon Pearl w/Zildjian cymbals

1... 7 x 14" Ludwig Snare Drum
2... 12 x 14" or 9x13" Tom-Tom
3... 28" Bass Drum
4... 14 x 16" Floor Tom
A... 12" Hi-hats

B... 12" Crash
C... 10" Choke
D... 13 or 15" Ride
E... 16" riveted Chinese Swish
F... 2 Cowbells

1941 Leedy catalog.

"The job of a drummer in a modern orchestra consists of two main divisions," Duke Ellington's long-time drummer Sonny Greer once wrote. "Firstly, to supply the basic foundational percussion; and secondly, to ornament or intensify the effects achieved by the other instruments. To foster this end we have a large assortment of instruments and gadgets, but given a dominant sense of rhythm, the only essential is a flair for 'effect' and a sense of rightness."

Greer was cofounder of Ellington's stylish band, setting his elegant tempo behind a massive array of percussion. "I made a deal back then with the Leedy Drum people, in Elkhart, Indiana," Greer once told jazz writer Whitney Balliett. "In return for my posing for publicity shots and giving testimonials, they

Duke Ellington conducts pal Sonny Greer at the Hotel Sherman, Chicago, 1940.

gave me a drum set that was the most beautiful in the world. Drummers would come up to me and say, 'Sonny, where did you get those drums? You must be a rich man,' and I'd nod. I had two tympani, chimes, three tom-toms, a bass drum, a snare—the initials SG painted on every drum—five or six cymbals, temple blocks, a cowbell, woodblocks, gongs of several sizes, and a vibraphone. The cym-

bals were from the Zildjian factory. I'd go out to Quincy when we were working in the Boston area, and one of the Zildjians would take me around. He'd tell me to choose cymbals with flat cups and instead of hitting a cymbal to show me how it sounded he'd pinch the edge with his fingers and you could tell just by the ring. I learned how to keep my drums crisp, to tune them so they had an even, clear sound."

In a 1933 article for *Melody Maker*, Greer wrote about his drums and their role in Duke's band. "I always maintain that the bass drum should be felt and not heard. Care should be taken that there is no 'ring' attached to bass drum notes.

"Personally I find the indirect action pedals the best...somehow even pedals of the same brand seem to possess personalities of their own.

"Next to the bass drum and the side (snare) drum, our most important asset is, I consider, the 'Charleston' or foot cymbals (hi-hats). I prefer the elevated type, as then the cymbals are also available for hand playing...on the subject of cymbals, I consider it impossible to give too much care to accents and dynamics.

"I personally use a pair of the tunable variety (of tom-toms), and whilst they are invaluable for 'jungle' effects, it is surprising the extraordinary facility with which they adapt themselves to other uses."

Summing up the bottom line in a typically scholarly fashion, Greer writes, "If a drummer cannot 'swing' a band, then he must perforce be adjudged a failure." In other words, "It don't mean a thing if it ain't got that swing."

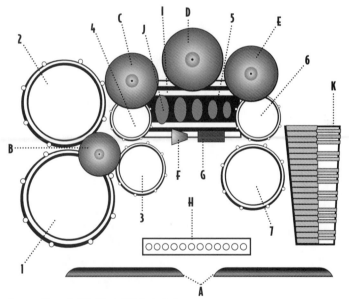

Sonny Greer's Kit Circa 1940...Leedy drums

1... 28" Tympani		**C**... 14" Crash	
2... 25" Tympani		**D**... 16" Chinese Crash	
3... 6½ x 14" Broadway Parallel Snare Drum		**E**... 14" Crash	
4... 8 x 12" Tom-Tom		**F**... Cowbell	
5... 28" Bass Drum		**G**... Woodblock	
6... 9 x 13" Tom-Tom		**H**... Orchestra Chimes	
7... 14 x 16" Floor Tom		**I**... Leedy Rollaway Trap Console	
A... 2 Gongs		**J**... 5 Tuned Temple Blocks	
B... 12" Hi-hat		**K**... 3 Octave Vibraphone	

Note: All drums in Marine Pearl with custom inlaid sparkle design. Cymbals, drums, and temple blocks all mounted on a Leedy Rollaway trap console.

Two "Kings of Swing," Davie Tough and Benny Goodman, in a 1938 Slingerland publicity still.

Courtesy Manny Wise

The little skinny guy from Chicago, Dave Tough, could take a set of drums and move an entire big band to swing like the reproductive regions of a bull elephant. Listen to Tommy Dorsey's "Song of India" and you'll hear the powerful simplicity of Tough's best attributes. He is the rhythmic guide that steers the band from the song's tom-tom based intro, right through the chorus and solos, bouncing merrily along in the background, all the while remaining steady as a Rolex. "So definite and swinging was his beat, so subtle were the little additions he made to color the arrangements, that in poll after poll, musicians of all kinds kept voting him their favorite drummer," wrote jazz critic George T. Simon.

Tough, who served as a musical mentor to Gene Krupa, among others, was a paradox of a man. Well read and spoken, he was known to chum around with Ernest Hemingway and F. Scott Fitzgerald. He also enjoyed the company of some of the finest jazz musicians of his day. Along with Dorsey, Davie Tough beat the skins for Benny Goodman and Artie Shaw. He found his niche with Woody Herman in the 1940s, matching his driving style with Herman's up-tempo charts. Reared on a steady diet of New Orleans drummers, Tough paid particular attention to the sound balance of his kit. He was a perfectionist about his drums, showing up early for gigs just to dampen the calfskin heads on his Radio Kings, permitting a warm, loose tone. He tuned his bass drum extremely low so as not to get in the way of the upright bass's notes. His cymbal work was particularly elegant, popping up in unusual and surprising places. Using two large bass-drum-mounted cymbals, along with a Chinese cymbal, Tough could accent passages, shifting dynamics at will, in order to establish a theme. Bassist Chubby Jackson said that Tough did "strange things to his cymbals. He'd remove all the (rivets) except one or two from his Chinese cymbal, and he'd cut a wedge out of a ride cymbal to get a broader sound."

Though Tough varied his cymbal arrangement only when recording, he apparently would rearrange his drums to fit the gig. When he played with Benny Goodman, Tough often played the traditional "Krupa" four-piece kit, with the large 28" bass drum and a 9 x 13" tom-tom on the drummer's left. Other times he could be seen using a smaller 7 x 11" tom-tom mounted on his right, along with the 9 x 13". Whatever the array of his set, Tough always used the right tools for the right job.

Frank Driggs Collection

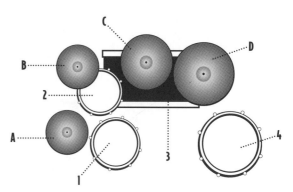
Dave Tough with his Radio Kings on an early 1940s recording session.

Rutgers Institute of Jazz Studies

Playing his big swish onstage in New York in the 1940s.

Courtesy Zildjian Co.

A dapper Tough checks out the metal at Zildjian in 1938.

Dave Tough's Kit Circa 1938...Slingerland Radio King drums, Marine Pearl w/Zildjian cymbals

1... 6½ x 14" Snare Drum	A... 12" Hi-hats
2... 9 x 13" Tom-Tom	B... 12" Thin Crash
3... 28" Bass Drum	C... 14" Chinese Swish
4... 16 x 16" Floor Tom	D... 16" Cymbal

Cozy works out some ratamacues on his brand-new Radio King.

Michael Ochs Archives

With rudiments flying off his sticks like sawdust from a chainsaw, Cozy Cole was the rhythmic and visual center of the famed Cab Calloway band in the late 1930s. His featured solo pieces on such tunes as "Crescendo in Drums," "Ratamacue," and "Paradiddle" conveyed to Calloway's audience the joy and power of drumming at its best. Cole became well known for his finely crafted solos, always deliberate in form and statement. "There's noisy loud and there's loud that sounds good," Cole once said in *Down Beat*. "You need taste and technique to make the drums sound like a musical instrument."

Taste is one characteristic Cozy had plenty of. His drums always sounded tremendously well balanced and well tuned. Cole is said to have been Sonny Greer's "band boy," an early predecessor to the drum tech. Like Greer, Cozy had an undying respect for the drum kit. He studied the instrument continuously, learning under such famous tutors as Billy Gladstone. Cole's commitment to drum education was so strong that he opened a drum school in 1954 with fellow sticksman Gene Krupa.

In 1957 Cozy scored a hit record with the drum-heavy "Topsy," an instrumental that crossed over onto rock and roll radio. In his liner notes for the drum anthology *Let There Be Drums*, Max Weinberg notes that "Topsy II" was "the first 'serious' rock and roll record to feature the drums."

During his career, which spanned seven decades, Cozy endorsed Ludwig & Ludwig, Slingerland, Rogers, Leedy &

Courtesy Rob Cook

100% Radio Kings for Cozy.

Courtesy Zildjian Co.

Testing cymbals in the Zildjian cymbal vault around 1968.

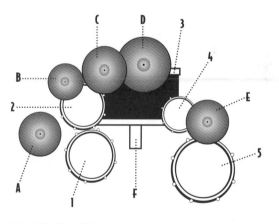

Cozy Cole's Kit Circa 1940...Ludwig & Ludwig drums, Avalon White Pearl, w/Zildjian cymbals

1... 7 x 14" Super Swing Snare Drum
2... 9 x 13" Tom-Tom
3... 26" Bass Drum
4... 7 x 11" Tom-Tom
5... 14 x 16" Floor Tom

A... 12" Hi-hat
B... 11" Choke
C... 13" Chinese Splash
D... 14" Crash
E... 12" Crash
F... Super Speed Pedal

Ludwig, and Pearl drums. With Calloway's band he employed two drum sets: a larger kit for the big band numbers, and a smaller outfit for the quintet features that the band would play during the show. In a Slingerland publicity shot from the 1930s, he is holding a Ray McKinley model Radio King snare drum, with a wooden top hoop and a flanged brass bottom hoop. A Ludwig & Ludwig ad from 1940 has him playing a 7 x 14" Super model wood shell snare. Author and vintage drum aficionado Rob Cook possesses a set of Leedys Cole once owned. The snare drum is a solid-maple shell Leedy & Ludwig made especially for Cozy.

"You must tune the set so it doesn't sound hard," Cozy told *Down Beat.* "And of course rhythm is very important."

Performing in London on a set of early 1950s Radio Kings.

Cozy in a Rogers publicity still.

Courtesy Chet Falzerano

Courtesy Zildjian Co.

1957 Leedy Advertisement

Ed Shaughnessy

1945-1960 Bop & Roll

Courtesy Zildjian Co.

Ellis Tollin

Andy Florio

Mel Lewis

Swing was still king in the early 1940s, but uptown in New York City, there were syncopated rumblings of change. A loose group of young musicians, whose base of operations was Minton's Playhouse in Harlem, was cooking up a new type of jazz. The music was dubbed bebop, and like most great artistic movements, it was a product of its era. America was gearing up for involvement in a world war in Europe and Asia. To supplement the war effort, new taxes and restrictions were placed on nonessential activities. Along with the dwindling of the big bands' ranks from an accelerated armed services draft, a dance tax was imposed that made it harder to keep the big dance palaces full of paying customers. The result, as Max Roach told *Modern Drummer*, was that "small groups had replaced big bands, dancing was prohibited because of the war tax, and musicians had to sustain the interest of the crowds with instrumental virtuosity."

The small bands gave birth to new stars of the drum set, players who rebelled against the traditional four-on-the-floor bass drum beat that had become the staple of the big bands. This fresh group of drummers, led by the great Kenny Clarke, chose to move the timekeeping emphasis over to the ride cymbal, using the snare and bass drum to punctuate the quick melodies and solos of instrumentalists like Dizzy Gillespie, Charlie Parker, and Thelonious Monk.

The American drum companies were not immune to the restrictions and sacrifices produced by World War II. A law decreeing that only 10% of a product's weight could consist of metal caused many of the drum manufacturers to radically change the design of their drums. Leedy, Ludwig, WFL, Slingerland, and Gretsch all created drums with imaginative solutions to the metal quotas. Hoops, lugs, and snare mechanisms that were normally made of metal were fabricated out of wood.

After the war, with the big bands in decline, musicians became journeymen. A typical drummer in New York

Les DeMerle

Max Roach

Art Blakey

NEW BROADKASTER "PROGRESSIVE JAZZ" DRUM OUTFIT $449

The latest, the finest in artist outfits for the progressive drummer playing with small groups. This is the exact outfit played by Art Blakey and by Max Roach on the Emarcy Records he made with his group. It's compact, strictly modern in appearance, and a pleasure to travel with. Note particularly the 20" x 14" bass drum (pioneered by Dave Tough and Gretsch) the 14" x 4" Max Roach snare drum (fastest sounding, snappiest answering snare drum you ever tried) and the 12" x 8" and 14" x 14" tom-toms so suitable for small jazz groups. Pictured here in Copper Mist Gretsch Nitron but also available in all other GRETSCH-PEARL and GRETSCH NITRON colors. See opposite page for detailed listing, finishes and price.

Gretsch Progressive Jazz Kit

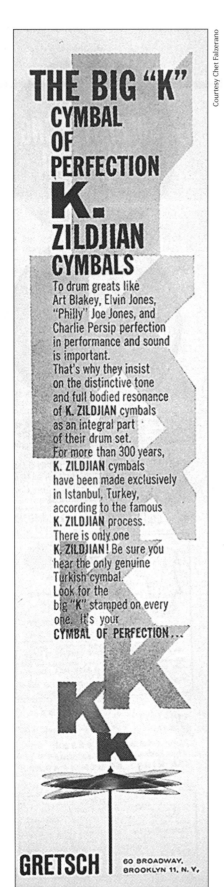

THE BIG "K"
CYMBAL
OF
PERFECTION

K. ZILDJIAN CYMBALS

To drum greats like
Art Blakey, Elvin Jones,
"Philly" Joe Jones, and
Charlie Persip perfection
in performance and sound
is important.
That's why they insist
on the distinctive tone
and full bodied resonance
of K. ZILDJIAN cymbals
as an integral part
of their drum set.
For more than 300 years,
K. ZILDJIAN cymbals
have been made exclusively
in Istanbul, Turkey,
according to the famous
K. ZILDJIAN process.
There is only one
K. ZILDJIAN! Be sure you
hear the only genuine
Turkish cymbal.
Look for the
big "K" stamped on every
one. It's your
CYMBAL OF PERFECTION...

GRETSCH
60 BROADWAY,
BROOKLYN 11, N.Y.

K. Zildjian Ad

Slingerland Ad

Andy Florio

may have had an afternoon recording date, followed by an evening club date, and finally an after-hours jam at another club across town. The cumbersome 28" bass drums and large tom-toms became outdated. Drummers needed a kit they could throw in the trunk of a taxi. In the late 1940s, drum makers began introducing smaller-sized drum kits. "It made it easier to get from town to town," said Max Roach. "Pack up your gear, put it in your car, and off you go....Plus, the bass drum had begun to become less and less an integral part of the whole musical setup." As the bass and snare drums became smaller, cymbals, the newest timekeeping elements, became bigger.

By the late 1940s, rhythm and blues, a spicy hybrid of blues and gospel music set to a swinging jazz shuffle, was gaining popularity. Many of the musicians came from a jazz background, then hopped over to rhythm and blues. The lines between jazz, rock and roll, and rhythm and blues were often blurred; Kenny Clarke played sessions with early rock-and-roller Joe Turner, as did the Modern Jazz Quartet's Connie Kay.

Rock and roll was the bastard stepchild of rhythm and blues and jazz, with a little country music thrown in. It scared the establishment just as much as bebop had done 15 years earlier. Its early practitioners, drummers like Fred Below, Panama Francis, Earl Palmer, and J.M. Van Eaton, took some of the best elements of jazz and adapted them to fit what they were playing. The beat was simplified, the rules were broken, and the way was paved for a very exciting period in the history of music.

Courtesy Zildjian Co.

Lilly Christine

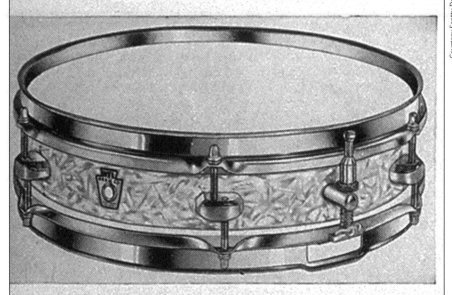

Courtesy Scotty Doucette

BUDDY RICH "BE-BOP" DRUM

The new "Be-Bop" style of drumming calls for a special 3"x13" snare drum and W.F.L. again leads with this new model.

It was designed at the request of Buddy Rich for use with small combos and on television shows. The smaller head area permits a crisp, sharp tone and resists head shrinkage caused by dry air conditioning and hot television klieg lights.

No. 905P—3"x13" Choice of Pearl, Chrome.................$55.00

WFL Buddy Rich Bebop Snare

The man who started it all.

The 3 Bosses—Klook, Pierre Michelot, and Bud Powell at the Blue Note in Paris.

If you take apart the essentials of what has been called bebop music, if you strip it down to its bare limbs, tossing away all the ornamentation, there alone stands Kenny Clarke's ride cymbal. Rhythmic, effervescent, and sly, it was the pulse of a revolution in music.

Clarke, or "Klook," as he was nicknamed, moved the drummer's traditional emphasis of time from the snare and bass drums over to the cymbals in order to form a more harmonious relationship in the rhythm section. Dizzy Gillespie traced the roots of bebop back to Klook. "We started getting into the new style of playing when Kenny Clarke came into Teddy Hill's band," Gillespie said. "Kenny really drew a different kind of sound out of those drums."

In the 1930s, Klook worked with his brother Frank, a bassist, to find a better way of driving a band than was the norm. "We worked a long time to find out how the rhythm men should 'play together'," he told writer Ira Gitler. "At that time, drummers played 'dig coal': they beat the snare drum like miners digging for coal. The bass players didn't like that....My brother liked [bassist] Jimmy Blanton a lot, and he thought that this style should be kept up by a light drummer who let the bass line be heard. That's how I started experimenting with the continuous cymbal line."

Clarke's new style of timekeeping alienated him from many of the musicians of the swing era who couldn't understand the

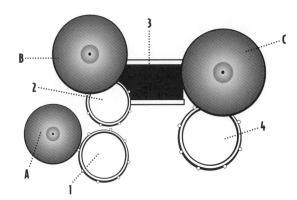

Kenny Clarke's Kit Circa 1956 ...Gretsch Broadkaster drums, Silver Sparkle, w/Avedis Zildjian cymbals

1... 5½ x 14" or 7 x 14" Snare Drum
2... 8 x 12" or 9 x 13" Tom-Tom
3... 22" Bass Drum
4... 16 x 16" Floor Tom

A... 15" Hi-hats
B... 20" Medium Crash Ride
C... 22" Medium Crash Ride

Note: Kenny used a tympani head on the bass drum batter side.

broken cymbal patterns and bass drum bombs he used to accent the music.

"I didn't care," Clarke said later. "I was young. I could play the way I wanted to play. I got fired for playing that way, but I kept on playing."

Klook formulated his new vocabulary on Gretsch Broadkaster drums and Zildjian cymbals. He also endorsed Trixon and Premier drums at one time or another. Some photos show him playing just an 18" ride and a set of 15" hi-hats, while a 1950s Zildjian catalog has him using 20" and 22" crash rides along with his 18" medium ride. In a sixties catalog showing his setup, he paired a 15" bottom hi-hat with a smaller 14" top in his endless search for a new and different sound.

Such was his love for music and learning that Klook aligned himself with the Premier Drum Company and opened a drum school in Paris in 1967. He was tireless in his efforts to educate a new generation of drummers. "The first principle of drumming is to find your sound; then let the technique come," he said. "Once technique becomes the master it distorts the sound of the drums; then it's useless."

"Kenny initiated a new language into the mainstream of jazz drumming," wrote Dizzy, "a new conception...which is now *the* dialogue."

Courtesy Chet Falzerano

"Real Swinger" Kenny in 1950s Gretsch ad.

Terry Cryer

Playing his Silver Sparkle Kit at the Club St. Germain, Paris, late 1950s.

He's more than just a famous jazz drummer. His playing has been a vital and important force in shaping the music of the last 50 years. Working both within and outside the traditional boundaries of the art form he helped to create, Max Roach is the drummer's drummer. His playing reminds us that the drums are a musical instrument, a potent rhythmic and melodic tool with a great and powerful legacy.

Since the 1940s, when he helped forge a new musical dialogue in jazz, Roach has taken the drums to more diverse places than any other artist. His lyrical drum solos have a vivid life of their own; humorous, cunning, intelligent, angry, and sorrowful, they run the range of human emotions. Roach seems to listen to and nurture the sound of his drums. He also realizes the importance of music as a tool for social change. His response to racial turmoil in South Africa and the U.S. in the early sixties prompted him to record *We Insist! Freedom Now Suite* with Abbey Lincoln, a blistering record of protest, invocation, and reaction. "I've never believed in art just for the sake of art," he told *Modern Drummer* magazine. "It is entertainment, of course, and dancing is also part of it, but it can also be for enlightenment."

Frank Driggs Collection

Three Deuces club, New York City, 1947.

Kenny Clarke was a great influence on the young Max Roach during the early years of bop. "[Clarke] was always accessible," he once said. "I got a lot out of Klook while he was in New York. I must have driven him crazy with my eagerness. But he was always ready to sit down with me and talk drums."

When a teenage Max recorded with Dizzy Gillespie, Charlie Parker, and Bud Powell in the 1940s, his sound on records was often kept in the back of the mix, due largely to the shortcomings of microphones and engineers in those days. His brilliant snare drum explosions are still evident, the staccato reactions to the fast melodies of his counterparts.

In the 1950s, Max teamed up with trumpeter Clifford Brown to record some of the best jazz that decade had to offer. His sound had become tighter, more focused. Gretsch dubbed its 4 x 14" snare drum the "Max Roach" model in honor of their famous endorser, touting its "crisper, faster response!" He also helped popularize the smaller "jazz"-size drum kits that became the standard set for the modern players. His bass drum sound

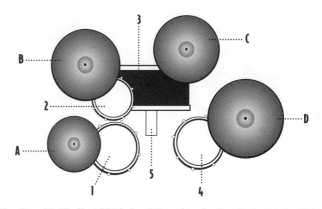

Max Roach's Kit Circa 1956...Gretsch drums, Silver Sparkle, w/Avedis Zildjian cymbals

1... 4 x 14" or 5½ x 14" Snare Drum
2... 8 x 12" Tom-Tom
3... 20" Bass Drum
4... 14 x 14" Floor Tom
5... Gretsch "Floating Action" Bass Drum Pedal

A... 14" top Hi-hat w/13" bottom Hi-hat
B... 18" Thin Fast Ride
C... 17" Medium Sizzle
D... 20" Medium Ride

Contemplating the future of jazz drumming.

from this period was melodic and tuneful, providing punch with tone.

Max used Zildjian cymbals along with his Gretsch drums in the 1950s. He experimented with a 14" top over a 13" bottom hi-hat, as well as a small-cup 18" fast ride. In the forties he played 15" hi-hats with an 18" and 20" or 22" ride cymbal.

"With the cymbals and other things, you can get a great deal of variety out of the drum set," Roach said in *Drums and Drumming* magazine. "...what you can do with the kit is endless. I don't think we've really scratched the surface yet."

Showing small jazz sizes in a 1950s Gretsch ad.

Professor Roach comparing tones.

A determined Art in the recording studio in the mid 1950s.

The Jazz Messenger caught in full swing.

I think I'm the least educated about the modern method of drumming than anybody in the field," Art Blakey once said. "I just play what I feel. I don't care if I got my sticks backwards, forwards— if I hear something that calls for me to use my elbow, I'll do it."

And do it he did. His drumming was a mighty mix of sound and swing, bubbling and boiling the pulse, using all the voices of the kit to state the essence of the rhythm. "Nobody can fill up a hole like Art Blakey," said Kenny Clarke. "He can put more rhythm into two bars than anyone."

Early in his career, Blakey had a drum act that featured a lot of stick twirling and other special effects. He wasn't getting the audience reaction he expected, so he enlisted the help of the great Chick Webb for some drumming pointers. Some years later he told writer Wayne Enstice what happened: "So Chick Webb say, 'OK kid, the first thing I want to tell ya: The rhythm ain't up in the air; it's on the hides.' So he said, 'You can roll?' I said, 'Sure Mr. Webb, I can roll.' He said, 'Well, roll.' I grabbed the drum and eh-eh-eh-eh. So he eased over to the door, and he looked at me [and] say, 'Shit.' Bam! Slammed the door and left me standing there."

"I learned, you know...you listen and learn. And I tried to do it just a little different."

Blakey's style was also forged in the drum chair for the Billy Eckstine band, a fiery pre-bop group that featured Charlie Parker and Dizzy Gillespie, among others. He later went on to play with many of the greats of bop before starting his own band in the late 1940s. The Jazz Messengers, which lasted until Blakey's death in

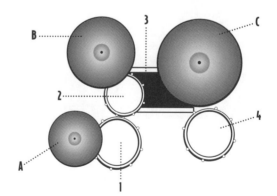

Art Blakey's Kit Circa 1955...Gretsch Broadkaster drums, Red Sparkle, w/K. Zildjian cymbals

1... 5½ x 14" Snare Drum
2... 8 x 12" Tom-Tom
3... 20" Bass Drum
4... 14 x 14" Floor Tom

A... 14" Hi-hats
B... 18" Medium Crash
C... 20 or 22" Medium Sizzle

ART BLAKEY...45

1990, was the launching pad for some of the finest musicians of the last 50 years; Hank Mobley, Clifford Brown, Branford and Wynton Marsalis, Wayne Shorter, Lee Morgan, and many others came of age in that roving university of jazz.

Blakey was the consummate Gretsch man in the 1950s, playing on a small Broadkaster "Progressive Jazz" kit. But it was the sound of his K. Zildjian cymbals that is most fondly recalled and sought after by drummers to this day. "Art was a true warrior," Lennie DiMuzio of Zildjian fondly remembers. "Even in his early days, he always liked big cymbals. They were usually K's; he loved that big, dark, funky sound."

Blakey would punctuate his bandmates' solos with those cymbals, never timid, always firmly in control of the group. "And if they get out of line," he said in *Down Beat* magazine, "you bring them back in, because that's what you're there for. You are the master of this whole thing."

Art Blakey plays Gretsch Drums

You can too. Try an outfit like Art's or specify your own set at your dealers. Write Gretsch, 60 Broadway, Brooklyn 11, N.Y. for Diamond Jubilee drum catalog. (This is our 75th year.)

1950s Gretsch ad.

Playing his Gretsches on a 1960s record date.

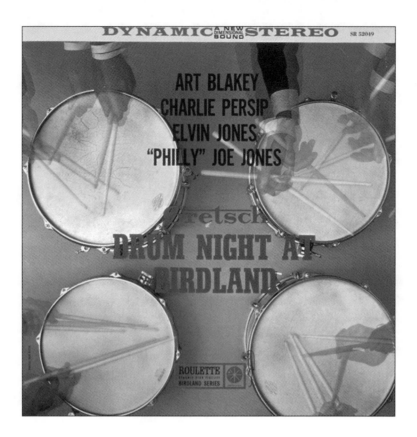

The phrase "That Great Gretsch Sound" was printed on a paper label inside every Gretsch drum. This was not an advertising slogan, it was a common belief shared by many of the bebop and big band jazz drummers of the 1950s. Max Roach, Charlie Persip, Philly Joe Jones, Shelly Manne, Elvin Jones, Don Lamond, Sonny Payne, Chico Hamilton, Art Blakey, Kenny "Klook" Clarke, Louie Bellson, Andy Florio, Art Taylor, and many more thought the sound of Gretsch was unique. So much so, that according to Duke Kramer, Sales Manager with Gretsch at the time, endorsers did not receive any compensation other than the drums that were given to them. In fact, they were required to turn in old sets before new ones were issued. "They just loved Gretsch so much," says Kramer.

Did Gretsch reinvent the drum? Was the sound of Gretsch drums truly unique? The answer is probably not, though much ado was made over the shell construction. Fred Gretsch was quite simply a marketing genius. He identified his drums with the passionate music of the day. (In fact, when Fred Gretsch was winding down his career, the company lacked the foresight to switch tracks to the exploding rock and roll craze, resulting in a dwindling market share.) Gretsch received support from their endorsers by being truly responsive to their needs and concerns. Company representatives Duke Kramer and Phil Grant periodically met with drummers in the clubs and asked their opinions and ideas on how to enhance the Gretsch product. Many improvements came out of these meetings, including the small (18" and 20") bass drums and 4" snare drums. These small kits became the benchmarks for the "Jazz" outfits that were dominant in that era's Gretsch advertising.

Another brilliant marketing move during the fifties was Fred Gretsch's fiercely competitive K. Zildjian advertising. Gretsch had been the sole importers of K. Zildjian cymbals for many years, from Constantinople (known as Istanbul after World War II), Turkey. Again, by closely associating themselves with a different concept, Gretsch capitalized on the loyalty and distinctive sound of their endorsers. Anyone hearing Art Blakey ride on one of his beloved K's will understand. Unlike Avedis Zildjian cymbals, with their consistent, machine-hammered sound, K. Zildjians were hand-hammered. Though this produced a distinctive tone, the inconsistency of hand-hammering led to many a "clinker." Nevertheless, Gretsch created quite a fervor in jazz periodicals with its "no parallel, no substitutions" advertising. With ad phrases like "Cymbal of Perfection" and "Look For the Big K," they caught the attention of aspiring jazz drummers around the world.

Fred Gretsch's brilliance in promoting his company is best evidenced in the famed "Gretsch Drum Nights" held at Birdland in the 1950s. These performances broke all attendance records at the famed New York club. Gretsch honored the occasion by having special sets made up, finished in "Cadillac Green," with gold-plated hardware and K. Zildjian cymbals. Philly Joe Jones, Elvin Jones, Charlie Persip, and Art Blakey traded four-bar solos on these memorable performances, which were recorded on Roulette records (now re-released on CD). In the 1950s, if it was jazz, it was Gretsch.

With Duke Ellington in the 1950s. Note the shallow tom-tom.

Courtesy Harry Cangany

Courtesy Zildjian Co.

A very sharp Mr. Bellson poses with his Gretsch drums at a Boston nightclub.

Louie Bellson has been there for all of it. He played with Benny Goodman at age 17, held the drum chair in Duke Ellington's band, beat the skins for Count Basie and Harry James, and toured with the prestigious "Jazz at The Philharmonic" troupe that included Ella Fitzgerald and Oscar Peterson. Oh, and by the way, he pioneered the double-bass-drum setup while he was still in high school.

"See," Bellson says, "I was a tap dancer when I was a kid. You'd learn how to do a time step and shim-sham-shimmy. That helped my drumming. I was also ambidextrous. They always had me up on stage at pep rallies, and the cheerleaders had me come up and play drums. I often wondered how it would be to have another big sound with the left foot besides the hi-hat.

"I sketched the first double-bass-drum idea in high school art class around 1938. My teacher, Mr. Faber, looked at it and asked me what it was, and I said, 'Well, this is a new idea for a drum kit with two bass drums instead of one.' Of course when I started that I didn't realize it would mushroom into quite a thing.

"About the time I did [the double-bass-drum setup], Ray McKinley came out with two bass drums. I guess both of us had the idea at the same time."

In those days, tom-toms were usually mounted on the bass drum rims, which was impractical for what Louie had in mind for his dream set. He wanted an 11" tom-tom on either side of

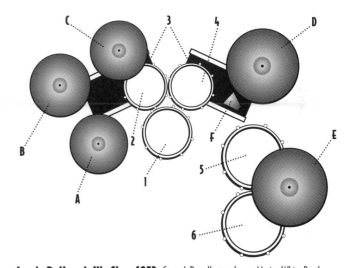

Louie Bellson's Kit Circa 1952...Gretsch Broadkaster drums, Marine White Pearl, w/Avedis Zildjian cymbals

1... 5½ x 14" Snare Drum		**A**... 15" Medium Hi-hats	
2... 7 x 13" Tom-Tom*		**B**... 16" Medium Ride	
3... 2 - 24 or 26" Bass Drums		**C**... 15" Medium Fast Crash	
4... 7 x 13" Tom-Tom*		**D**... 19" Medium Swish	
5... 16 x 16" Floor Tom		**E**... 20" Medium Ride**	
6... 16 x 16" Floor Tom		**F**... Cowbell	

*The tom-toms were custom-made to a 7" depth. "I didn't want to reach too high to hit them," says Bellson.
**Later on, Louie piggybacked a riveted China Boy underneath this ride cymbal.

Louie in a 1960s Rogers publicity shot.

two 13" tom-toms, somehow suspended over the two 20" bass drums. To this end, he put a very deep 16" floor tom between his two bass drums to anchor the smaller toms. "I was trying to get a connection by putting up that big tom-tom in the middle to hold up those 9 x 13" and 7 x 11" tom-toms on either side. Then I discovered that even with a 20 x 20" bass drum, I had too wide a span and my legs got tired after a while from that stretch. I got rid of that big tom-tom in the middle and just put one 9 x 13" tom-tom on each bass drum. I always wanted to make sure my time elements [cymbals] were in a place where I could reach them, because we were playing fast tempos in those days. You couldn't have a ride cymbal five feet away from you or you'd be lost in the shuffle."

When Bellson became Benny Goodman's drummer, he was a Slingerland endorser, having won a nationwide talent search in a Gene Krupa drum contest. "When I joined Benny, the manager told me Benny had a contract with Gretsch, but at 17 years old I was afraid to go up and say, 'Hey Benny, I'm sorry, but I play Slingerland drums.' He wouldn't have said a word, but I was a green kid and I didn't want to disrupt him at all, so I moved over to Gretsch."

Bellson stayed with Gretsch through the 1950s, playing his double-bass-drum kit with Duke Ellington's band. "Duke was like a

second father to me," he remembers fondly. "With Duke, I learned not only about drums, but also composition from him and Billy Strayhorn.

"I listened to everybody when I was growing up, from Baby Dodds on down to Chick Webb and Zutty Singleton. Then along came Jo Jones. To me he was one of the greats, because he picked up from all those other guys and played with Basie, and you know how that band was. They were swinging so hard!

"And Big Sid Catlett taught me a lot too. There's a guy who was so big, you'd think he'd have a rough touch, but he could play that Chinese cymbal better than anybody. He would play it so it had a musical texture to it. I learned from Big Sid and those guys how to really ride on that China Boy cymbal."

Which brings to mind another subject close to Bellson's heart: cymbals. "I like to have about three or four different ride cymbals for all the different colors. I don't like to ride on one cymbal, it gets too boring. The China Boy with the six rivets is my 'Dizzy Gillespie' cymbal; Dizzy used to carry one of those all the time. He'd give it to the drummer he was playing with and say, 'I don't want to tell you what to play, but you play this for me.'"

Louie has lasted a long time in a business that is notorious for shortening the employment of its practitioners. He still enjoys

Showing Wayne Newton a few tricks.

A rare photo of one of Louie's first double-bass setups. Notice the extra-large floor tom in the center.

doing clinics and teaching the next generation of drummers the wisdom that he has gained in his long career. "Jo Jones and Sid Catlett used to show me things and say, 'Now pass it on.' You've got to pass on all that beautiful heritage.

"First of all you have to believe in yourself. Put your mind to having fun working and sweating. Make sure you know your craft. Even though I'm 70 years old, I'm just starting to learn."

Listening to a playback.

"New Orleans is always known to produce good swinging drummers and trumpet players," says Earl Palmer, legendary session musician and one of the founding fathers of rock-and-roll drumming. Palmer was part of a group of New Orleans musicians that formed the backing band for trumpeter and producer Dave Bartholomew in the late 1940s. They rose to prominence when they appeared on early recordings by the great Fats Domino, as well as other Crescent City acts.

In the fifties, producers would travel to New Orleans with such stars as Little Richard and Sam Cooke to benefit from the magical groove that Palmer and his fellow musicians were laying down at J & M studios. "It was just a natural feel we had, I didn't have to make any adjustments. What I was doing was what they wanted." The irresistible feel and energy of those sessions produced some truly ground-breaking rock and roll: "I'm Walkin'," by Fats Domino; "Long Tall Sally" and "Keep a-Knockin'," by Little Richard; and "Tipitina," by Professor Longhair.

"I was influenced by guys like Big Sid Catlett and Buddy Rich. What I liked about Rich was the only thing he couldn't do was what he couldn't think of. And Big Sid was so versatile, which is what I consider my forte. Also, I was a tap dancer in New Orleans in the French Quarter for tips. My mother and aunt were in vaudeville.

"What I used to try to do before rock and roll became totally a straight-eighth-note feel, I used to think in terms of how

EARL PALMER
West Coast Recording Artist

EARL PALMER'S
AVEDIS ZILDJIAN CYMBAL SET-UP
A. 15" New Beat Hi-Hats
B. 18" Crash Ride
C. 20" Ride (Medium)

A Zildjian diagram showing Earl's 1960s setup.

[Louis Jordan's drummer] Christopher Columbus would play that shuffle and afterbeat [backbeat]. I was a hell of a lot younger then. It didn't bother me at all if they wanted something really fast. Long as it's fast and it's exciting and it's steady, then you get a good take. If they'd want it faster, I'd say, 'You want it fast or do you want it to swing?'

"Some of the older stuff I did with Dave Bartholomew, I had an old, old set of Leedys. The bass drum had a picture of a nude woman on it. I didn't know anything about Zildjians or anything, so I went and bought some cymbals; they sounded like garbage can tops. Dave [Bartholomew] screamed bloody murder, said, 'Man, if you don't get that shit outta here!' and gave me some money to go get some cymbals.

"Then I got a set of Gretsch drums and the drummer in Sherman Williams' band gave me two Zildjian cymbals that I still use to this day.

"In those days my drums were [tuned] considerably loose, except for my snare. It was loose, but I put a wallet on it to get a good, flush, afterbeat sound. Nobody was using matched grip back then, so you'd have to hit the rim and the drum to get a good afterbeat."

In 1957, Palmer moved to Los Angeles, spending the next two decades as one of the most-recorded session men in the business. His drumming graced literally thousands of sessions with such diverse artists as Ike and Tina Turner, Lawrence Welk, The Righteous Brothers, and Bonnie Raitt. "The reason I was there was my versatility. I found out by being able to play different concepts; jazz, rhythm and blues, rock and roll, cajun, and all that is the big reason I was so busy.

"After I came to California I never used nothing but metal snare drums. It was always a Ludwig metal snare drum. See, with metal snares you get a good snare sound and it's crisp. You can't get a wooden snare drum to sound like a metal drum, but you can sure get a metal drum to sound like a wooden one."

Palmer's key to his laid-back sound follows a simple philosophy: "Don't overplay. Think in terms of keeping time with that instrument and making it swing. Relax with it, play it as if you've been playing it all along. That helps it groove a lot better."

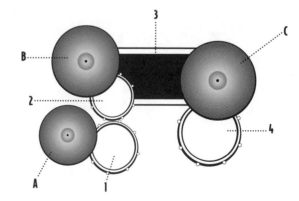

Earl Palmer's Kit Circa 1956...Gretsch Broadkaster drums w/Avedis Zildjian cymbals

1... 6½ x 14" Snare Drum	**A**... 15" Hi-hats
2... 9 x 13" Tom-Tom	**B**... 18" Crash
3... 26" Bass Drum	**C**... 20" Medium Ride
4... 16 x 16" Floor Tom	

Philly Joe on a 1960s record date.

Ray Avery Archives

"**D**rums can be played with the bass drum, snare drum, and ONE cymbal," Philly Joe Jones told *Down Beat* magazine in 1960. "...if you don't have the cymbal, you can use the snare drum. I know a lot of guys can sit down and play just the snare drum."

Always pushing ahead, always caring for and loving the music he played, Philly Joe was a dynamic drummer who could pulse an entire band with just a ride cymbal. He had a melodic, musical, and energetic approach to his craft, following the examples set by Kenny Clarke and Max Roach. His fiery cymbal and snare-drum work were also the perfect counterpoint to such strong players as Hank Mobley, Pepper Adams, and John Coltrane. His work

Giving the set a good workout.

with Miles Davis in the 1950s reveals a sophisticated artist unafraid of making a strong rhythmic statement. "Philly Joe was the fire that was making a lot of shit happen," writes Miles in his autobiography. "...I left a lot of space in the music for Philly to fill up. Philly Joe was the kind of drummer I knew I had to have."

Philly came to the public eye during his stint with Miles, but he also recorded with some fine bands that he fronted. The true Philly Joe Jones can be heard on these recordings. He conveys a complex sense of musical interplay between the instruments and an unrelenting enthusiasm for the composition.

Like many of the great drummers of his time, Philly Joe was reared on a strict diet of swing drummers. He took the best attributes of the big-band drummers, such as taste, power, and style, and adapted them to modern jazz. "Sid (Catlett) was very close with me, he liked me," Jones said. "I got most of my brush work from him. Sid used to sit down and show me the things I wanted to know."

Philly also got something else from Big Sid. When Catlett died, he willed his favorite cymbals to Jones.

Following the lead of many jazz drummers of the fifties, Philly played Gretsch drums, augmenting his 20" bass drum with an 8 x 12" tom-tom and a 14 x 14" or 16 x 16" floor tom. His famous lightning-quick cymbal work was executed on K. Zildjian cymbals, which gave him plenty of stick clarity and the warm-colored tones he sought to convey his distinctive image of time and rhythm to the world.

In New York during the 1950s.

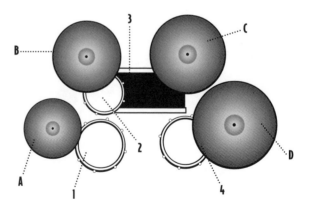

Philly Joe Jones' Kit Circa 1957...Gretsch Broadkaster drums w/K. Zildjian cymbals

1... 5½ x 14" Snare Drum
2... 8 x 12" Tom-Tom
3... 20" Bass Drum
4... 14 x 14" Floor Tom

A... 14 or 15" Hi-hats
B... 18" Ride
C... 20" Medium Heavy Ride
D... 22" Sizzle (optional)

Roy playing a WFL "Bebop" snare drum in the studio.

Popsie Randolph/Frank Driggs Collection

Working his magic on the hi-hat.

When Roy Haynes sits down at his drums, the sounds he makes are among the most distinctive in all of jazz. He has the boundless energy of an exploding galaxy, taking rhythmic invention and swinging it to a new stratosphere. His cymbal work is defined by precision and clarity, while his snare drum approach is pointed and lyrical. His talents have been sought by what seems to be a "Who's Who" of twentieth-century jazz: Lester Young, Charlie Parker, Miles Davis, Ella Fitzgerald, Sonny Rollins, John Coltrane, Sarah Vaughan, Chick Corea, and Pat Metheny. Through it all, Haynes has maintained a purity of vision that makes his playing timeless and unique.

"I've always had a different, personal way of doing things, like holding drumsticks," he told *Modern Drummer* magazine. "I'm not a run-of-the-mill person or player. People are just getting hip to many of the things I've tried to do on drums."

Listen to Roy in many different contexts and you'll understand what he means. On his 1958 debut as a bandleader, *We Three*, Haynes summoned the same seasoned authority he would use three decades later in another trio setting, 1990's *Question & Answer*, where he teamed up with bassist Dave Holland

Roy Haynes' Kit Circa 1952...WFL drums, Marine White Pearl, w/Avedis Zildjian cymbals

1... 4 x 14" Compacto model Snare Drum
2... 8 x 12" Tom-Tom
3... 20" Bass Drum
4... 14 x 14" Floor Tom

A... 14" Medium Hi-hats
B... 15" Thin Fast Crash
C... 20" Medium Ride

and guitarist Pat Metheny.

In the 1940s and fifties, 52nd Street in New York was the center of the jazz world, and Roy Haynes was always there, ready to take any gig that came his way. He soaked up knowledge from some of the greats, taking ideas and adapting them to fit his drumming. "Max [Roach] was using only one cymbal," he told Ira Gitler, "keeping time on that with the right hand, his left hand accenting on the snare drum, and his foot instead of kicking 4/4 was also used for accents like another hand. After I saw him, I got rid of my tom-toms and used only one cymbal."

In the fifties, Roy used a small WFL Buddy Rich "Bebop" model snare drum and a 20" bass drum with a 12" rack tom and a 14" floor tom. "I was one of the first drummers to use very small snare and bass drums. One critic said, 'Roy Haynes has a small snare drum because he's a small guy.' That's so ridiculous. I got the small drums because I had a small sports car and they fit in the trunk!"

Roy's trademark cymbal sound is the result of using flatter-profile rides with a good, specific stick sound. "Most of the cymbals that

Courtesy Scotty Doucette

Photo taken during a brief stint with Slingerland.

Roy uses are tight," says Zildjian's Lennie DiMuzio, a long-time Haynes friend. "He likes a lot of definition. He's got an incredible ride beat with lightning speed and lots of clarity."

Haynes says one of the reasons he plays flat rides is for the "inner feeling" the cymbals have. "You won't get a lot of resonance, but you can feel it coming up through the bottom.

"When I was learning, and I feel I'm still learning, I used to practice until I got tired," Haynes told *Down Beat* in 1959. "I don't like to play on a pad. I like the feel of the skins and the cymbals, and the sound of the drums."

1956 taping at ABC in Los Angeles.

Shelly Manne was what you might call a "late bloomer" on the drums, having started playing at the ripe old age of 18 years. Of course, most students aren't lucky enough to have the legendary drummer Billy Gladstone as their first instructor, as Shelly did. "I'll never forget that first lesson he gave me," Manne told *Modern Drummer* in 1984. "Billy put me in that room downstairs at Radio City Music Hall where they kept all the percussion instruments. He showed me how to set up the drums I got and how to hold the sticks. Then he put Count Basie's 'Topsy' on the phonograph, and as he walked out of the room, he said, 'Play!'"

Manne was a quick study, and in a few short months he was playing his first professional gigs. By the time he joined Stan Kenton's band in 1946, he had already subbed for Dave Tough with Benny Goodman and recorded with Coleman Hawkins and Dizzy Gillespie. His swinging, tuneful style made him extremely popular with musicians and listeners alike.

With Kenton's band, Manne flourished and grew into a star in

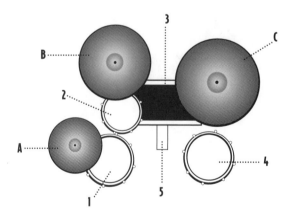

Shelly Manne's Kit Circa 1954...Gretsch Broadkaster drums, Ebony Finish, w/Avedis Zildjian cymbals

1... 5½ x 14" Snare Drum	**5**... Gretsch "Floating Action" Pedal
2... 8 x 12" Tom-Tom	**A**... 14" Medium Hi-hats
3... 20 or 22" Bass Drum	**B**... 19" Medium Thin Crash Ride
4... 14 x 14" Floor Tom	**C**... 22" Medium Ride

Playing Gretsch-Gladstones with the Stan Kenton Band.

I LOVE MY *Leedy* DRUMS

MORE THAN "ANYTHING"

SHELLY MANNE

IF YOU WANT THE BEST
BUY *Leedy*
send for our latest catalog
LEEDY DRUM CO.
CHICAGO 48, ILLINOIS

Shelly as a teen idol in 1960s Leedy ad.

his own right. In 1952, he moved from New York to Los Angeles to explore the new California jazz scene. He quickly became identified as the main drummer for the West Coast Sound, a hybrid of cool jazz and bebop soloing concepts that was evolving into an important counterpoint to the hard bop of the East Coast. "I realized that drums could be used as a melodic instrument and still maintain their place in the rhythm section," Manne said of that period. "Instead of letting the rhythm imply its own melody, my concept is to play melodically and allow the melody to create rhythm."

"He didn't seem to become a homogenized player like so many players do," says the great jazz drummer and percussionist Larry Bunker of his friend. "To this day if I hear something on the radio, within four bars I know if it's [Shelly]. He had the ability to find the right thing to do in virtually any situation while still sounding like Shelly."

Manne used Gretsch-Gladstones in his early days as a drummer, then went to a Gretsch Broadkaster jazz kit in the 1950s. One of his prized possessions was an original custom-made Billy Gladstone snare drum given to him by his mentor as a gift.

In 1957 he became the main endorser for the revived Leedy Drum Company, now on its last legs as a budget line owned by Slingerland. Manne was one of the first drummers to play a drum

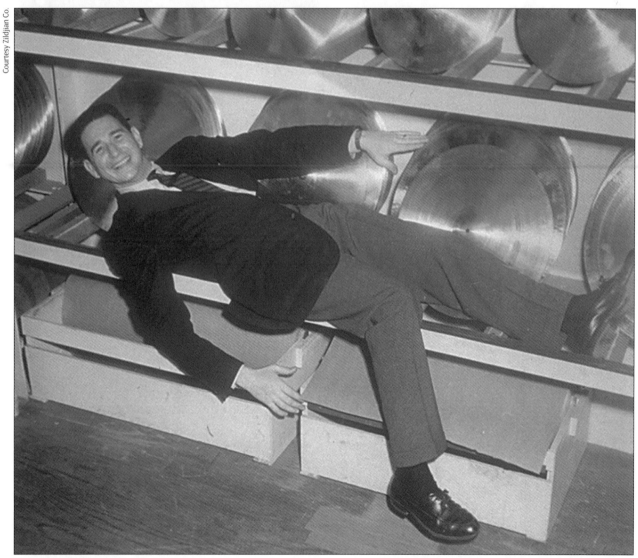

Having a snooze in the Zildjian cymbal vault.

kit that had a natural wood finish, something for which he caught flack from Leedy owner Bud Slingerland, who felt that Shelly should be seen playing the more expensive pearl-covered sets. "I said, 'Look, Bud, I find that pure wood sets get the best sound for me; I just like the way they resonate.' So he said, 'I'll make them.' And you know, they became a big seller for Leedy."

Manne's fondness for cymbals came partly from his deep admiration of Dave Tough's work on the bronze discs. "The power he could generate within a group and the way he splashed cymbals...I just knew that it moved me.

"I try to get a cymbal that doesn't set up a definite pitch. I try to get an even-sounding cymbal that doesn't spread too much. I don't want a cymbal that builds up if I'm not putting more energy into it." To this end, Manne often used a flat-top ride cymbal for its stick sound and lack of dominating overtones.

Hammering out some details with Avedis Zildjian.

The drum set was an important tool for Shelly, but technical virtuosity was secondary to a good set of ears. "Technique is only a means to get there.... The main thing a drummer still needs to do is play time that swings....The time has to live, not just be good time. A metronome has good time."

Connie Kay Sonor Ad

1960s THE NEW FRONTIER

Jake Hanna

Ludwig Rock Ad

Vox:
it's
what's
happening
to
drums

Now Vox puts percussion
in shape. In fact, three
groovy shapes—
standard, conical
and elliptical. All with
fabulous new features and
sounds. Like the double pedal
timpani effect of the elliptical
bass. The wild, new croco nylon
finishes. The faster, easier
adjustments—no screwdriver
ever needed. The most compact,
fold-up construction. On stage they're
loud, crisp and sparkling. In the studio: clean,
precise, fresh. Makes them the toughest
trio to beat in the business. Whatever your
bag, you'll get better sounds on Vox
drums, the sound at the top. See them now at
your nearest Vox dealer. Once you beat 'em,
you'll want to join 'em.

Vox Drums

In the early 1960s, music was changing as fast as the world around it. The traditional structures of modern jazz were beginning to erode and mutate as musicians began questioning the established roles of their instruments. Ornette Coleman showed up in New York with a plastic saxophone and set the jazz world on its ear. John Coltrane, fresh from playing with Miles Davis, formed a band that affected the next generation of players the same way Charlie Parker had done 20 years earlier. Near the decade's end, Davis himself, always the innovator, fused jazz with rock and funk instrumentation and made electric what was once acoustic. Jazz music would never be the same again.

Pop music was also undergoing great changes. The enormous success of rock and roll in the mid 1950s spawned an entire industry devoted to the sole purpose of making hit records. The music, which was

DRUM WITH THE SMILE BUILT IN!

Rogers

dyna·sonic

• no snare slap

• no beats running
together

• no choking

• no distortion

• yes amazing!

• full power plus
beautiful sound

• try it

METAL OR PEARL
5" x 14", 6½" x 14"

Rogers DRUMS

Rogers Dynasonic Ad

The World's Finest Since 1623

AVEDIS ZILDJIAN

Zildjian Ad

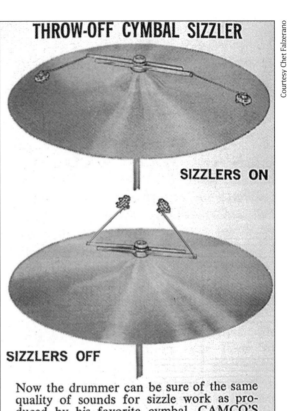

THROW-OFF CYMBAL SIZZLER

SIZZLERS ON

SIZZLERS OFF

Now the drummer can be sure of the same quality of sounds for sizzle work as produced by his favorite cymbal. CAMCO'S new THROW-OFF CYMBAL SIZZLER can quickly be adjusted to all sizes up to 22" in a few seconds. Note the square sliding arms which enable the drummer to place sizzlers at the desired distance from the edges.

No. 730 price $3.00

THE CAMCO DRUM ACCESSORIES CO.
9221 South Kilpatrick Avenue
P. O. Box 554   Oak Lawn, Illinois
Phone GArden 3-2900

Camco Cymbal Sizzler

SLINGERLAND DRUMS
played by BARRETT DEEMS
with JACK TEAGARDEN

SLINGERLAND
BARRETT DEEMS

BARRETT DEEMS
The World's Fastest Drummer
with Jack Teagarden

Barrett's career started years ago with famed Joe Venuti which later included the Dorsey Bands, Louis Armstrong, Recording, T.V. and European Tours. Currently he is with Jack "Big T" Teagarden, a fantastic group made up of the finest jazz names in the business.

Barrett has held the esteemed honor of drummers everywhere as being the "World's Fastest" and a showman of highest caliber. It's only natural that his drums are SLINGERLAND—known the world over to be manufactured with the built-in quality. Barrett states "Slingerland Drums provide the serious drummer with the extra edge of self-confidence and satisfaction."

Write for your free 4 color catalog today.

SLINGERLAND DRUM CO.
6633 Milwaukee Ave.   •   Niles 48, Illinois

March 29, 1962 • 47

Barrett Deems Ad

once considered deviant, now became the main-stream money maker for the record business. Session players became a hot commodity, developing an identifiable sound for singers, producers, and songwriters. Rhythm sections like the ones associated with Motown, Stax, Phil Spector, Muscle Shoals, and Nashville were setting a pulse the whole world could dance to.

None of this was lost on the English. Across the ocean, in Liverpool, Manchester, and London, young musicians with a deep reverence for the blues and R&B were getting ready to conquer the world with

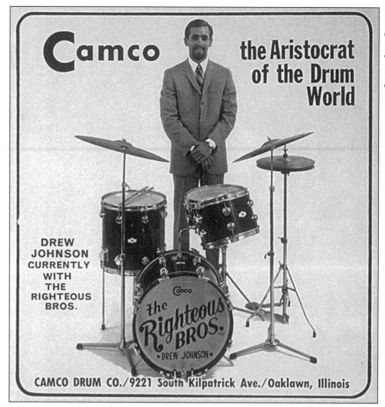
Camco Ad

Geo. Way Drums

Ludwig Ad with Ed Thigpen

their interpretation of American music. The sounds created by the Beatles, the Rolling Stones, Led Zeppelin, and the Who would travel across the Atlantic and in turn influence the new crop of American bands.

Drum companies also enjoyed great prosperity in the 1960s. While Gretsch was still associated with jazz, Ludwig, Slingerland, and Rogers all benefited from what drum historian John Aldridge has called "The Ringo Effect". The drum makers boosted production to keep up with the high demand created by the British Invasion. In an effort to stay current, they introduced new "hip" finishes and sturdier hardware geared towards the heavy-hitting rockers. European drums like Premier, Sonor, Trixon, Ajax, Hollywood, Olympic, and Vox made significant inroads into new markets. Another important change in the drum set was the addition of a second bass drum and multiple tom-toms. While not a new concept, the extra drums added new voices to a music that was relying more and more on amplification.

Near the end of the sixties, the focus in rock music started shifting to the instrumentalists, giving drummers a chance to stretch out and experiment with new ideas and sounds. The interplay between guitar, bass, and drums pioneered by Ginger Baker, Mitch Mitchell, Carmine Appice, Keith Moon, and John Bonham harkened back to the glory days of bebop, proving yet again there is nothing new under the sun.

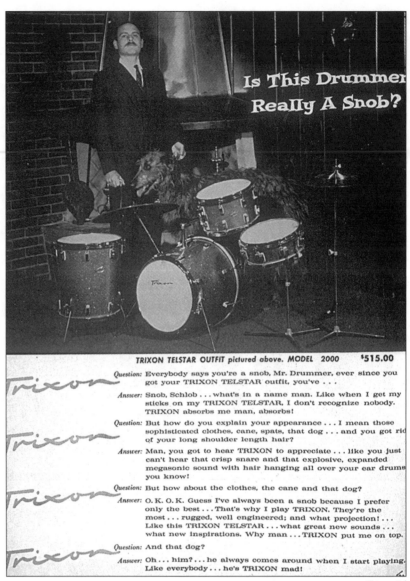

Trixon Ad

Premier Ad

Camco Advertisement

The Monkees

Connie Kay

In the recording studio in the mid sixties.

Rutgers Institute of Jazz Studies

Popsie Randolph / Frank Driggs Collection

Playing in a New York nightclub, late 1950s.

Elvin Jones is a man clearly in love with his drums. He approaches the kit as a singular musical voice, stretching and molding time, blurring the lines between artist and instrument. Although traditional influences can be heard in his music, Jones departed from convention and created his own unique style of drumming. He is one of a select few musicians, like Baby Dodds, Kenny Clarke, and Billy Cobham, whose playing is so original, it changes the course of everything that follows after it. "My drums are my life," Jones told Whitney Balliett. "Sometimes what happens to you during the day affects your ability and shows up in your work. But once you get to your set, you can obliterate all the troubles, which seem to fall off your shoulders."

Elvin grew up in Pontiac, Michigan, the product of a large family that also yielded jazz pianist Hank Jones and composer Thad Jones. Although he was not formally trained, he advanced quickly, adapting ideas he culled from people like Jo Jones, Sid Catlett, and Gene Krupa. "I just picked things up as I went along," he said in *Down Beat*. "It all boils down to a lot of hard work and midnight oil. You just have to listen and learn and try to relate the things you hear to your own way of playing."

After paying his dues in Detroit, and flunking an audition with Benny Goodman in New York, Jones worked with Charles Mingus, Bud Powell, and Harry "Sweets" Edison before finally hooking up with saxophonist John Coltrane in 1960. The pairing of Jones and Coltrane, along with bassist Jimmy Garrison and pianist McCoy

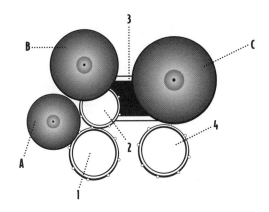

Elvin Jones' Kit Circa 1965...Gretsch drums, White Satin Flame, w/K. Zildjian cymbals

1... 5½ x 14" Snare Drum
2... 8 x 12" Tom-Tom
3... 20" or 18" Bass Drum
4... 14 x 14" Floor Tom

A... 14" Hi-hats
B... 18" Crash
C... 20" or 22" Riveted Ride

Conjuring the elements behind his Gretsch drums.

Tyner, would revolutionize jazz music by freeing up the constraints of solo and compositional forms. Jones' drumming was the perfect foundation for Coltrane's stream-of-consciousness saxophone style. The album *A Love Supreme* put the Coltrane band at the forefront of a new type of jazz. Jones' playing on the record is nothing short of astonishing. His drums are like an entire percussive orchestra, rolling and tumbling majestically through the music in powerful waves of sound. "Of all the bands and all the people I've worked with, the six years with [Coltrane] were the most rewarding," he told Balliett. "It seemed that all my life was a preparation for that period."

The Elvin Jones sound is a classic example of the "It ain't the drums, it's the drummer" rule. His the ability to pull the most out of his drums and cymbals is a result of hitting them with great conviction and skill. During the sixties and seventies he played the requisite Gretsch jazz-sized drums and K. Zildjian cymbals. "I found that I didn't need the heavy timbre of, say, a 24" bass drum," he told *Modern Drummer* in 1982. "All I needed was something that would be felt throughout that small group. And through a little experimentation...I could get the same depth out of that small bass drum as I could a larger one. It's simply a matter of tuning." Jones keeps his front head tighter than his batter head to "control the pitch of the instrument without losing any of the tonal consistency."

Jones strongly believes in utilizing the many sounds available on the drum kit to summon the strong emotions in his music. "Everything that's included in a drum set is there for a purpose and should be learned. Whether you use it consistently or not, you should know how to use it."

It's hard to imagine what the 1960s would have been like without the Beatles. The Fab Four not only revolutionized the music business by setting trends in songwriting and producing, they consistently reinvented popular music with each album they released. Their sound was both easily identifiable and difficult to define, a mixture of rhythm and blues, rock and roll, with a little Music Hall and Broadway thrown in for good measure. They were capable of playing the sweetest love song on one track, and then switch gears, breaking out the distorted guitars and heavy drums on the next cut.

Ringo Starr, the man who put the beat in the Beatles, was one of the most influential drummers in the sixties, inspiring thousands of kids to pick up the drum sticks for the first time. His playing style was deceptively basic and straightforward, exactly what the music called for. But behind the simplicity lurked a crafty inventiveness.

During the filming of *Help!*

Listen to the way he approached songs like "Tomorrow Never Knows," "Rain," and "Come Together." He heard the essentials of a tune and then came up with a drum part that perfectly served the song.

John Lennon, George Harrison, and Paul McCartney all were frustrated drummers and often suggested a certain rhythm to Ringo who would then adapt it to his style. "...the three of them each had their own idea of what the drummer should do and then I had my idea," Ringo told *Modern Drummer*. "So all I would do was combine my idea, their three ideas...They got what they were given and it worked."

Ringo played Ajax and Premier drums in the very early Beatle days, but moved on to Ludwigs when he started making some money. "I loved Ludwig drums. Premier I felt were too heavy, Gretsch were too fast for me, and Ludwig just seemed to be the ones I could get real good tones out of and they were good for my style of playing."

Ringo's popularity was extremely good for the Ludwig company. "Not long after the Beatles 1964 appearance on the Ed Sullivan show, Ludwig was forced into double shift production, primarily to

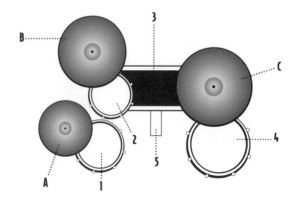

Ringo Starr's Kit Circa 1966...Ludwig Super Classic drums, Oyster Black Pearl, w/ A. Zildjian cymbals

1... 5 x 14" Jazz Festival model Snare Drum
2... 9 x 13" Tom-Tom on a Rogers Swiv-o-matic mount
3... 22" Bass Drum
4... 16 x 16" Floor Tom
5... Speed King Pedal
A... 14" Hi-hats
B... 18" Medium Thin Crash
C... 18" or 20" Ride

Other equipment included: Atlas snare stand, WFL hi-hat stand, two model #1400 cymbal stands and a Porto-Seat stool. Special thanks to John Sheridan.

With the legendary Oyster Black Pearl Kit circa 1965.

keep up with the demand for Oyster Black pearl drum sets," says John Aldridge, vintage drum expert and author of *A Guide to Vintage Drums*. "Due to the popularity of Ringo and the Beatles, there are probably more Oyster Black pearl kits 'out there' than any other color manufactured by Ludwig in the sixties."

In keeping with the simplicity of his playing, Ringo used a minimal amount of cymbals. "He's got a set of cymbals that he's used for a long, long time," says Jeff Chonis of Drum Paradise, who drum teched for Ringo on two solo tours. "They sound fantastic. When we set them up for the first time, Ringo said to me 'These are *the* cymbals, guard 'em with your life.' "

"It's a personal choice," Ringo said in *Modern Drummer*, "but I feel Avedis [Zildjian] is the best cymbal—an old Avedis. I love old cymbals."

"He likes his toms and kick tuned to a low range," says Chonis. "He likes his snare tuned fairly low, but not so low you can't get a good crack out of it, because he does play rim shots, has for a long time. So it still cracks, but it's got a lot of snare spray and a lot of low end."

"Top of the Pops, 1966."

"I tuned the drums for how I wanted them to sound in front of me," said Ringo in Max Weinberg's book *The Big Beat*. "I'd tune them and then go up to the booth and listen while someone played them for me."

For the sessions that yielded the *Abbey Road* album, Ringo chose to go with two rack toms instead of one. He used a natural maple Ludwig kit with calf heads. "*Abbey Road* was tom-tom madness...I went nuts on the toms," he told Weinberg. "The kit made me change, because I changed my kit."

Joe listening to playback in studio.

Listening to Joe Morello's drumming is like watching Michael Jordan play basketball. Like Jordan, Morello plays with such great style and finesse that he makes the technically impossible seem simple and unassuming. Pianist Marian McPartland called his drumming "a precise blend of touch, taste, and almost unbelievable technique." This is the guy who made 5/4 swing so hard on Dave Brubeck's jazz classic "Take Five" that the song bounced right onto the charts and into the hearts of thousands of fans around the world.

Joe became a WFL endorser in 1953 when he was with McPartland, but he played Ludwigs long before that. His first drum kit was a black lacquer Ludwig hand-me-down that he got from his cousin. "I went with Ludwig because I always really liked the drums," he says. "A lot of European companies like Premier, Trixon, and Sonor approached me about endorsements when I was with Brubeck, but I was happy over at Ludwig. They made a great product. Bill Ludwig Jr. was one of my dearest friends. As a matter of fact, he was my best man when I got married."

In the late 1950s Ludwig was competing against Gretsch and Slingerland for the jazz drummers' market, and having Morello as their keystone endorser was a big asset to the company. They featured him in numerous ads and promotions and sold many a silver sparkle kit as a result. Morello played his crisply defined snare patterns on a Ludwig Supra-phonic 400 and a Super Sensitive. The drums were made of chrome-plated brass at the time, and helped define the sound of modern jazz. Today Morello endorses D W drums and Sabian cymbals.

...matching the modern style of Joe Morello— LUDWIG...most famous name on drums!

Ludwig the drum standard of the world for tone quality and craftsmanship!

Hip couple "digging" Joe's silver sparkle Ludwigs.

At a time when most jazz drummers were playing smaller-sized sets, Morello chose to go with a 22" or 24" bass drum, 13" mounted tom-tom, and a 16" floor tom. "Playing an 18" bass drum is like playing a floor tom," he says; "it just isn't my thing."

Joe lays down the gospel onstage in London with the Brubeck band.

Overstatement about equipment isn't Joe's thing either. On the subject of cymbals he offers practical advice. "Cymbals are cymbals. There's good ones and bad ones," he says. "You just try to get something you're happy with. I always loved Dave Tough's playing with Woody Herman's band. He brought out that big cymbal and really started riding on it."

Joe played Zildjians during his years with Brubeck, but endorses Sabian these days. He prefers a 20" ride with either a 17" or 18" crash. His hi-hats can vary between 12" and 14".

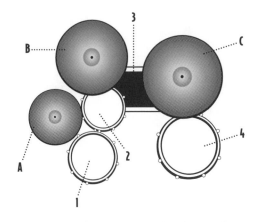

Joe Morello's Kit Circa 1960...Ludwig drums, Silver Sparkle, w/Zildjian cymbals

1... 5 x 14" Supra-phonic 400 Snare Drum   **A**... 14" Medium Hi-hats

2... 9 x 13" Tom-Tom   **B**... 19" Medium Crash Ride

3... 22" Bass Drum   **C**... 21" Medium Ride

4... 16 x 16" Floor Tom

More drums than you can shake a stick at.

In the studio with the monster kit.

Even to the most jaded observer, the honors that Hal Blaine has accumulated in his career as a session drummer are nothing short of astonishing. Over 350 Top Ten records, 40 Number One records, and 8 Grammy Records of the Year were graced by his groove. Turn on a radio station that plays the hits of the sixties and seventies and chances are you'll hear Hal's playing more often than not. He was

the anchorman for producer Phil Spector's famous "Wall of Sound" records like "Be My Baby" and "He's a Rebel." Classic tunes like Elvis Presley's "Return to Sender" and "Can't Help Falling in Love," "California Girls" and "Good Vibrations" by The Beach Boys, Simon and Garfunkel's "Bridge Over Troubled Water" and "Mrs. Robinson," "A Taste of Honey" by Herb Alpert, "California Dreamin'" by The Mamas and the Papas, and Frank

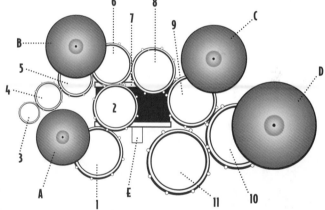

Have Fun!!! Play Drums!!!

Hal Blaine's Monster Kit Circa 1969...Ludwig Classic drums, Blue Sparkle, Custom-made fiberglass Tom-Toms, w/Avedis Zildjian cymbals

1... 5 x 14" Ludwig Supra-phonic 400 Snare Drum
2... 9 x 13" Ludwig Tom-Tom
3... 6" Single-Headed Tom-Tom
4... 8" Single-Headed Tom-Tom
5... 10" Single-Headed Tom-Tom
6... 12" Single-Headed Tom-Tom
7... 22" Bass Drum
8... 13" Single-Headed Tom-Tom

9... 14" Single-Headed Tom-Tom
10... 16" Single-Headed Tom-Tom
11... 16 x 16" Ludwig Floor Tom
A... 14" Hi-hats
B... 16" Thin Crash
C... 17" Sizzle with one Rivet
D... 22" Medium Ride
E... Rogers Pedal

Note: The fiberglass toms were mounted on two adjustable wheeled movie light stands made by Rick Faucher.

Full view of the monster kit.

Sinatra's "Strangers in the Night" all bear the mark of his tasteful playing. He was the "ghost" drummer for The Monkees, The Partridge Family, The Archies, The Carpenters, and The Beach Boys. If you wanted a hit record in the 1960s, you hired Hal Blaine and The Wrecking Crew.

The Wrecking Crew was a loose group of studio musicians who had worked together on the Phil Spector records at Gold Star Studios in Hollywood. The "Wall of Sound" was just that; crowds of players crammed into the studio creating what Hal calls "a state of barely controlled chaos." The musicians became in-demand gold makers, highly sought after by record companies hungry for a hit.

An "anything goes" attitude pervaded the Spector sessions. "We experimented a lot in those days," recalls Hal. "I had several big toy boxes full of every kind of percussion you can imagine. We would pull out shakers, jingle bells, and anything that would

Young Hal fronting his own band in Lake Arrowhead, CA, 1945.

Performing at "Hal Blaine Day," October 1991, Holyoke, Mass.

work on a song. I made the first 'ching ring' I ever heard by fitting a tambourine with a dowel and a hi-hat clutch. Every time the hi-hat would close, I'd get a tambourine afterbeat."

Hal stayed busy in the studios for many reasons. He always played the right part for the song, concentrating on feel and dynamics, never letting ego get in the way of a good take. He's quick with a joke or story, putting people at ease with his humor and good vibes and treating everybody with the respect that he feels they deserve. When a young and green Jim Keltner was just starting out in the studios, Hal was there to give encouragement and support. "Hal was extremely nice and put me at ease," writes Keltner in the foreword to Hal's memoirs. "I also felt that I could ask him anything without feeling like a dodo."

Hal explored different techniques in his hunt for new drum sounds. "The surf [music] thing was real big and Terry Melcher and Bruce Johnston were doing all that stuff over at Columbia," he remembers. "Terry wanted to get some kind of a different tom-tom sound. I started experimenting with the timbales, loosening them up to get a nice decay or fall-off sound. So I mounted the small one on the bass drum and put legs on the big one and used it as a floor tom."

Producers fell in love with the tones the timbales made and began specifically asking for Hal to bring the kit to sessions. "I was getting such great sounds with them, I started thinking 'Gee, if I had a whole mess of these I could really do some great fills.' I

started working with my drum guy, Rick Faucher, who's great with mechanical stuff, and Howie Oliver, a builder in L.A., and we experimented with various tube sizes for the drums. We made them out of spun fiberglass and put Ludwig hardware on them. Howie came up with the idea to use Klieg light stands for the mounting system. The idea was to augment a regular four-piece Ludwig kit, where I could still reach every tom-tom with no problem. The toms would just roll right in, one set on the right and one on the left."

The setup, which featured seven single-headed toms, ranging in size from 6" to 16", became known as "The Monster Kit", and soon took the drum world by storm. Ludwig took Hal's idea and created the "Octaplus" kit, which became one of the drum company's best-selling outfits.

Hal's method of tuning the eight tom-toms is typically creative. "I start at the bottom and play 'I Got Rhythm' on the toms and tune it up from there. It was a fun kit to play because of the great fills you could do on it. There were never fills like that because there were never drums like that."

When asked to name a song that best represents his drumming style, Hal mentions "Up, Up, and Away" by the Fifth Dimension and "MacArthur Park" by Richard Harris. "I was lucky, because I got to a point in my career where people just trusted me. There were so many records where they let me be me."

Benny Benjamin with other Motown players in the Joe Hunter Band.

Courtesy Martha Reeves

The sign above the awning on the unassuming little house about a mile from General Motors headquarters in Detroit pretty much summed it all up: Hitsville USA. Better known as Motown, the building was the epicenter of scores of Top Ten hits in the 1960s. From a tiny studio in the basement of 2648 West Grand Boulevard, a small group of writers, arrangers, musicians, and vocalists were producing gold records the way the big Detroit automakers were pumping out cars. Artists like Smokey Robinson and The Miracles, Marvin Gaye, The Supremes, The Temptations, Gladys Knight and the Pips, Stevie Wonder, and The Four Tops all relied on a secret ingredient for that magical "Motown Sound": The Funk Brothers. Anchored by the leadership of pianist Earl Van Dyke, the Funk Brothers were the house rhythm section Motown depended upon to make their hits cook.

Uriel Jones with James Jamerson on bass in a Detroit nightclub, 1964.

"They used to say you could get a chicken, and put that rhythm section behind him, and squeeze him to make him squawk, and it'd be a hit," says Uriel Jones, who, along with Benny Benjamin and Pistol Allen, played drums on many of the Motown hits.

"We were jazz-oriented, Earl Van Dyke and all of us. We were into Miles and Charlie Parker and those guys. The old giants."

Benny Benjamin was a supremely gifted drummer, who had the ability to cut to the essence of an arrangement and find the right groove. It was Benjamin, Van Dyke, and legendary bassist James Jamerson who really created and perfected the Motown feel, but Jones and Allen were often called in to substitute for the sometimes unreliable drummer. "Benny had a reputation as kind of a screwup," says Jones, "but he had that sound so they put up with it. Smokey [Robinson] was the first one who got mad at Benny and said 'Hey, I ain't using you no more!' That's when I started doing all Smokey's stuff like 'Second That Emotion.'

"You couldn't be too different [from Benjamin]," says Jones. "Regardless of what you wanted to play on the part, if you couldn't play like Benny, you wasn't gonna do the session. We copied Benny just as close as we could. They had established this rhythm and they didn't want to mess with it.

"We was cutting so many tunes, and they were coming out so fast, it's hard to remember who played what song. If I hear them now, I can tell the difference between Benny, Pistol, and myself. Pistol was the shuffle expert. He'd drive you up the wall with that shuffle, a real steady grind."

Jamerson's solid melodic bass playing was the true soul of the band. "He would really bring it out of you," says Jones. "Boy, he had a feeling!

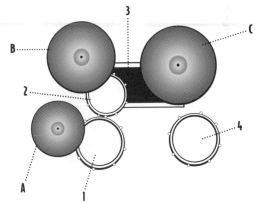

Benny Benjamin playing a red sparkle Rogers kit in 1961.

Motown's Kit Circa 1967...Ludwig and Slingerland drums, Red Sparkle Pearl, w/Zildjian cymbals

1... 5 x 14" Slingerland or Ludwig Metal Snare Drum

2... 8 x 12" Mounted Tom-Tom

3... 20" Bass Drum

4... 14 x 14" Floor Tom

A... 14" Hi-hats

B... 18" Crash

C... 20" Ride

One of the kits at the Motown studio was a mixed WFL and Rogers setup in black diamond pearl. Uriel Jones says this was used infrequently in the isolation booth for overdubs.

"When we started, there wasn't but one mike on all the drums. The rhythm section didn't use any isolation booths unless we were dubbing in or something. We would sit in that studio, and it was like a circle; everybody was facing everybody and the producer was right in the middle. There was just something about that room."

Motown's producers and arrangers were always looking for new ways to texture sound. One of the methods they used to achieve a rich, full drum sound was to have two drummers playing on a song. Jones remembers that the first time double drumming was used on a session, it was more out of necessity. "I don't remember the song, but Stevie [Wonder] came in there with a tune and Benny couldn't play the rhythm. It was so unorthodox. Stevie played it for you and you'd look at him and he'd sound like an octopus. I tried it and I couldn't play it. So he split it up; Stevie told me to do one part and told Benny to do another.

"We didn't do too much tuning in those days. We used the same heads for years, so the sound didn't really change. The sets consisted of different kinds of drums, like Slingerland and Ludwig. It was never more than four drums. The snare drum was a metal drum, a Slingerland I think. The small tom was 8" [deep] and the floor tom was a 14". It was a bebop kit. It wasn't a great big bass drum, it was a small one.

"Benny would always pawn his drums. One time they called him in for a session and the pawn shop was closed, so he used what he had, which was a hi-hat, a snare drum, a ride cymbal, and a stick and a brush. The record did well when it came out and for the next six months, a lot of the sessions were with that set. If you couldn't do it like that, you wasn't gonna work."

Motown studio A—Where it all happened.

Drummer Pistol Allen playing behind Joe Williams.

Uriel Jones in the 1960s.

Collection of the Author

Courtesy Annie Jamerson

Ludwig Hollywood outfit.

The Ludwig Drum Company rose to the top of the industry in the 1960s. After having operated from 1937 through 1954 as the WFL Drum Company, William F. Ludwig Jr. and his father, William F. Ludwig Sr., purchased the Ludwig & Ludwig name from Conn in 1955. This coincided with the birth of rock and roll and helped to give Ludwig a very competitive edge over other American drum makers. They regained the rights to lug designs, model names, and the historically significant Ludwig name, in addition to the product lines they'd offered since 1937 under the WFL brand. With the merger of two drum lines that had previously been direct competitors, and the return to family ownership of the Ludwig name, the Ludwig Drum Co. was poised to take the lead in drum manufacturing in the United States.

The top endorser for Ludwig in the 1950s was Buddy Rich. Although Buddy was the most technically proficient drummer to have made it into the national focus, Slingerland still ruled the drum world with Gene Krupa as their star endorser. Both of these drummers would fade from the public view as rock and roll began to replace big band music in popularity with the younger generation. The Beach Boys, Elvis Presley, Jerry Lee Lewis, and Buddy Holly and the Crickets were drawing America's youth into the next wave of popular music, and a lot of the drummers played Ludwig drums.

Another factor that helped increase Ludwig's name recognition was the advent of school music programs and the popularity of youth drum and bugle corps. By pursuing and helping to pro-

mote percussion instruments in an educational setting, Ludwig gained a lead early on in the sight of student musicians. The focus placed on education by the *Ludwig Drummer* publications also helped to reinforce the already prominent use of Ludwig drums in the schools. I remember dreaming of one day owning a Ludwig drum just like the ones the high school band in my hometown used, and later played on Ludwig drums almost exclusively in every band situation I encountered throughout junior high, high school, and the colleges I attended.

One of the most significant influences on Ludwig Drums in the 1960s, and drum set sales in general, was Ringo Starr. When Ringo appeared on the Ed Sullivan show in 1964, Ludwig received so many orders for drums it had to go into double shift production.

Another important factor in the success of Ludwig in the sixties and beyond was the Supra-phonic 400 snare drum. Based on the Standard model design that Ludwig had used from its inception in 1909 until the late thirties, the "Super Ludwig" as it was first called in the early sixties has proven to be one of the best all-around snare drums ever built. Almost every drummer worth his salt had a "400" behind his set regardless of the brand of tom-toms and bass drums used. This still holds true today with many major recording artists and studio drummers. Undoubtedly the most-recorded snare drum of the sixtie's and seventies, the Ludwig Supra-phonic 400 is still influencing the designs of drum makers around the world.

Playing in London.

Ian Dickson

Eric Clapton watches as Baker thunders ahead.

Bob Gruen / Star File

Ginger with Luwigs in 1968. Note the Leedy snare and the Rogers tom mounts.

Ginger Baker marches to the beat of no drummer but himself. "I've never really listened to any rock and roll drummers at all," he says. "I don't listen to anybody else. I only listen to what I'm working on."

Fiercely independent and always relevant, Baker has maintained his position on the forefront of drumming's vanguard for more than 30 years. From his days with Cream and Blind Faith to his collaborations with avant-garde producer Bill Laswell, Baker consistently redefines the drum kit and the way it is played.

His thundering sound stems from his drums, usually a large Ludwig kit with more than a healthy share of Zildjian cymbals. He was one of the first rock drummers to use a double-bass-drum setup. "I started playing two bass drums in 1966 with Cream. I got the idea from seeing people like Louie Bellson with Duke Ellington. That's what really got it in my head." Baker is self-deprecating when people say he influenced a whole generation of rockers with his double bass drumming. "That just goes to show how sick the world is," he says.

"I'm using that same silver sparkle Ludwig kit I used with Cream on the sessions I just did with Jack Bruce and Gary Moore," he says. "Although now I use 20" bass drums instead of 22". I still use the same 22" riveted ride and 14" hi-hats that I got from Zildjian in 1966, which says something about Zildjian quality."

Baker's favorite snare drum is a 1940s vintage 5" Leedy snare drum. "I got it from Kid Ory's drummer when they were touring in England around 1960. It's an old wood shell drum with the straight rims," he says. "I've done in a lot of sticks on those rims."

When asked if his drums were ever dampened for any recordings, Baker is typically resolute. "Nobody ever muffles my drums!" he says flatly. On tuning he offers this advice, "You tune the tom-toms to a chord, in tune with the bass player and the guitar player. You listen to the rest of the band and make them sound good," he says. "That's what a drummer's job is."

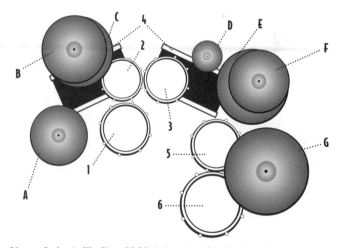

Ginger Baker's Kit Circa 1968...Ludwig drums, Silver Sparkle, w/Zildjian cymbals

1... 1940s 5 x 14" Leedy Snare
2... 8 x 12" Tom-Tom w/Rogers mounts
3... 9 x 13" Tom-Tom w/Rogers mounts
4... 2 - 22" Bass Drums
5... 14 x 14" Floor Tom
6... 16 x 16" Floor Tom
A... 14" or 15" Hi-hats

B... 17" Medium Thin Crash
C... 18" Medium Thin Crash
D... 8" Splash
E... 19" Medium Ride
F... 16" Medium Crash
G... 22" Medium Riveted Ride

Note: Ginger piggybacks cymbals B over C and F over E.

Onstage in New York with the Doors.

Don Paulsen/Michael Ochs Archives

Ringo Starr

Bob Gruen/Star File

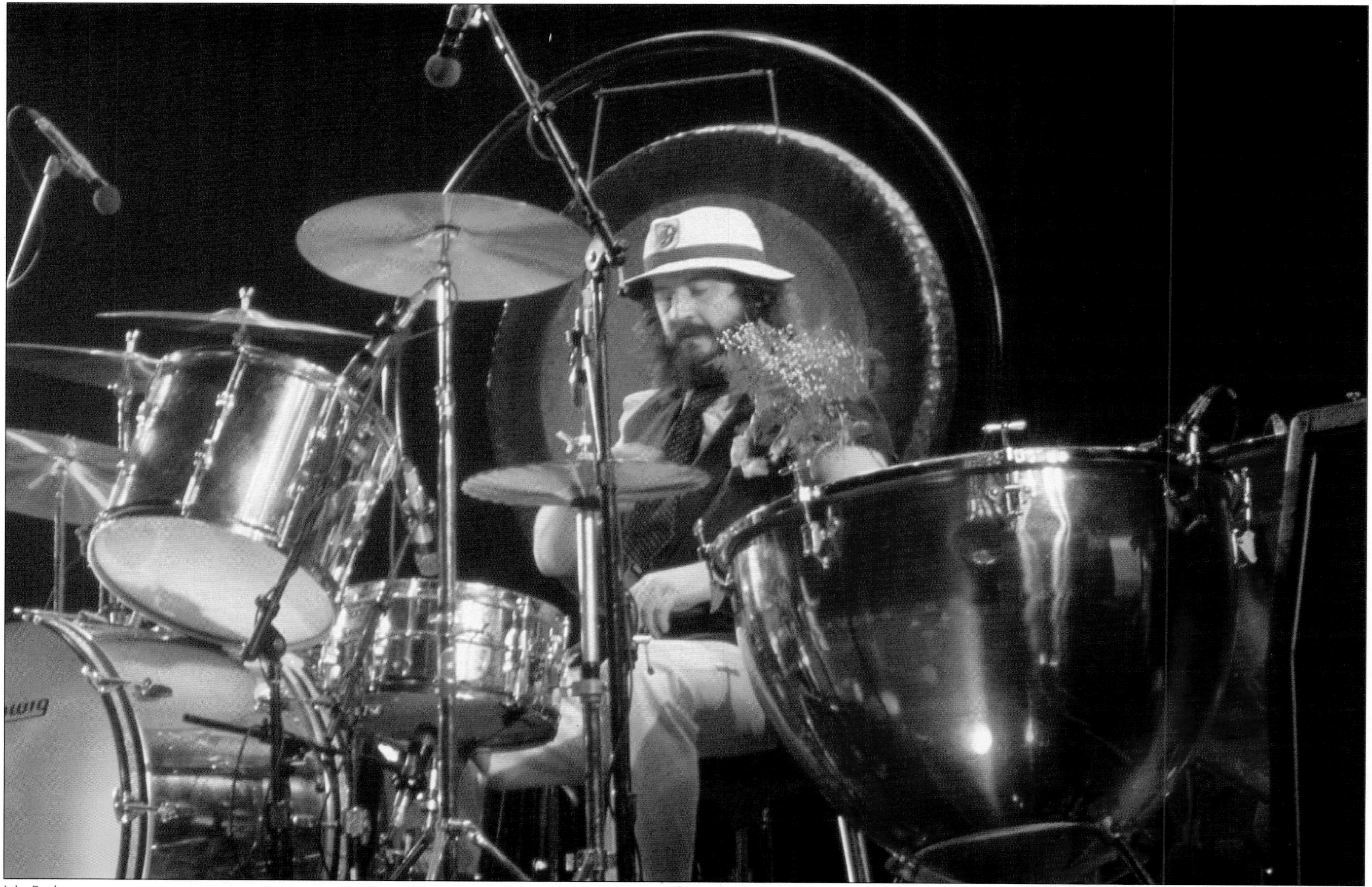

John Bonham

Jeffrey Mayer

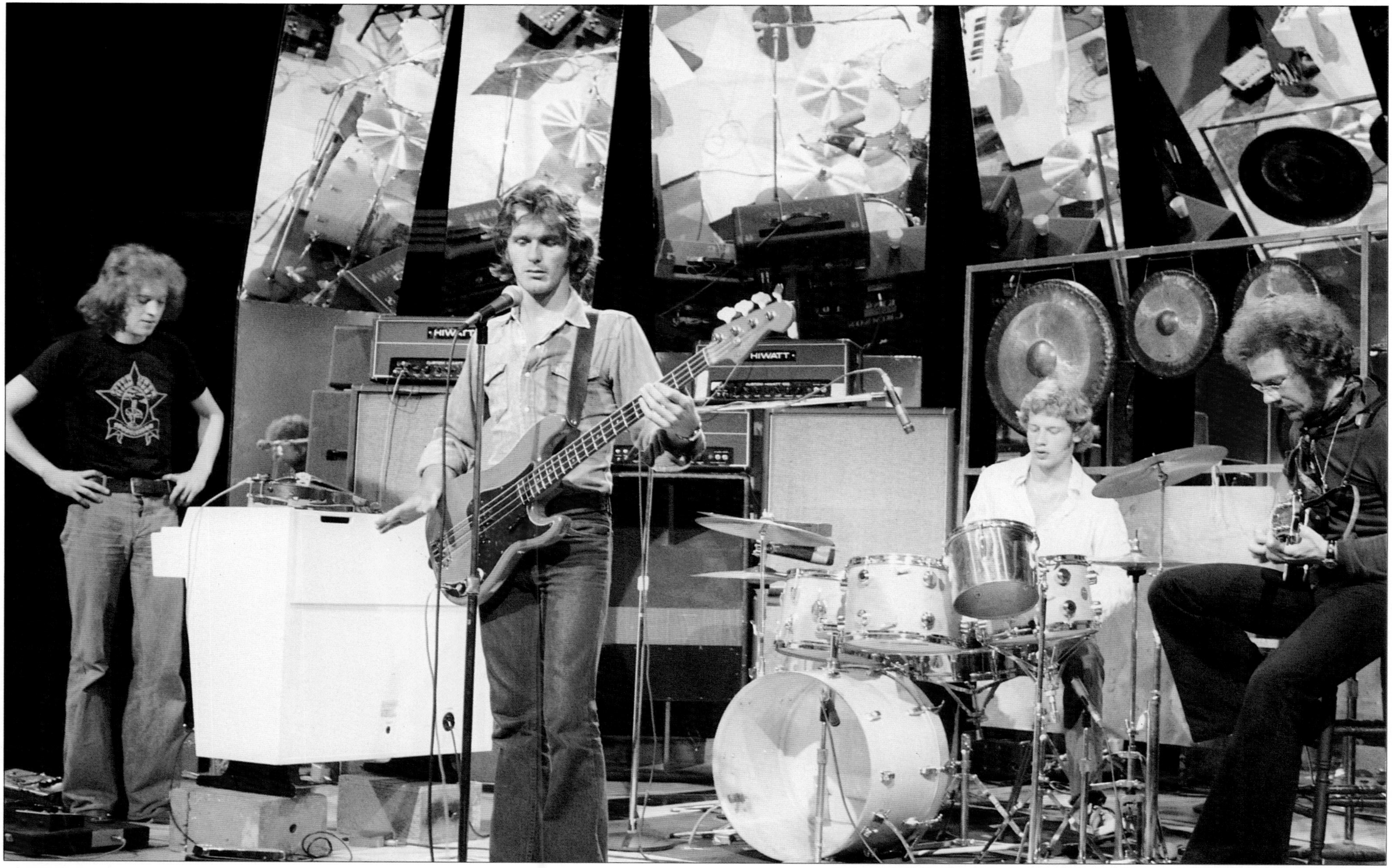

Bill Bruford

Jeffrey Mayer

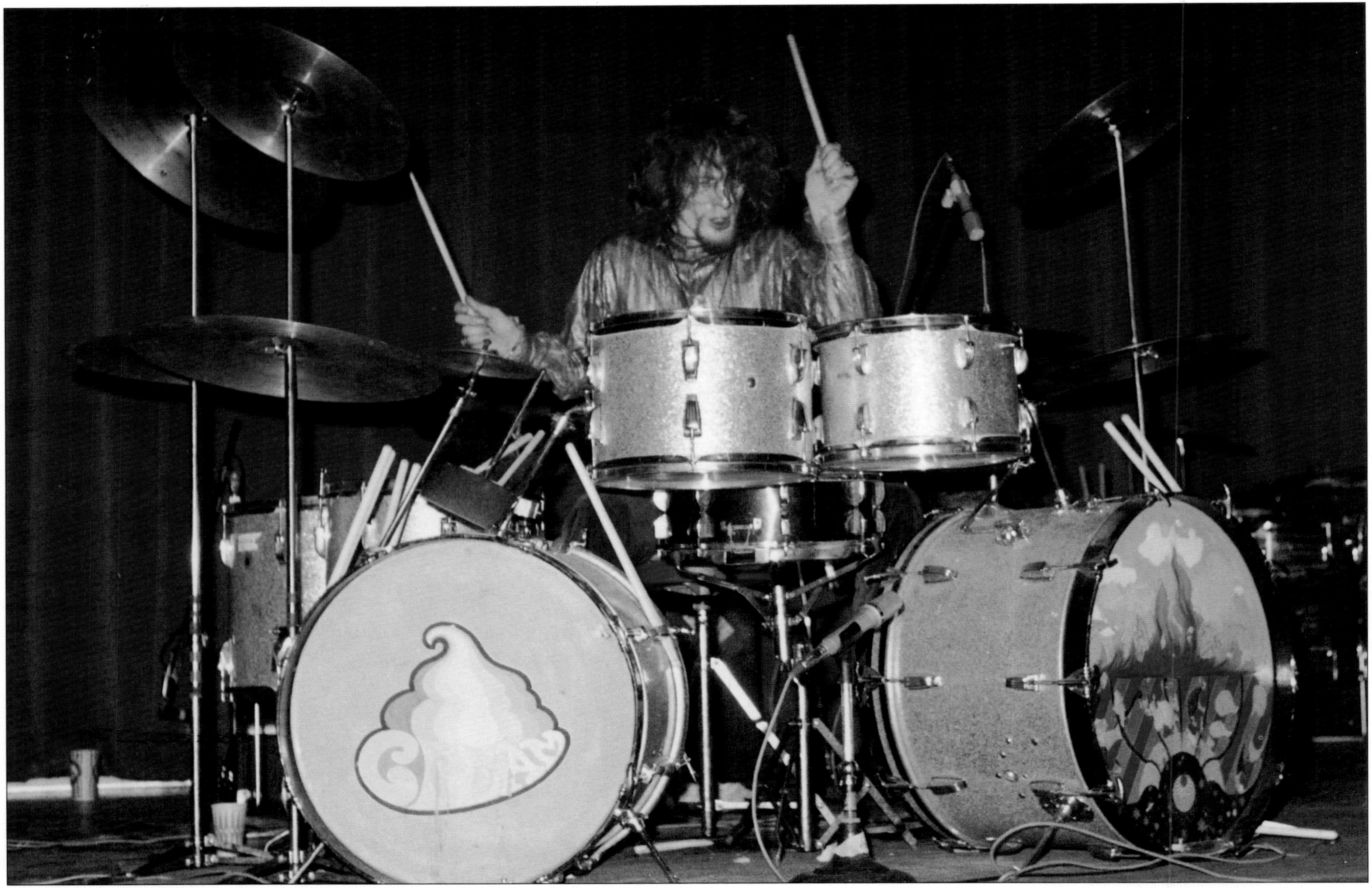

Ginger Baker

Joe Morello's 1960s Ludwig Set.

Photo by the Author

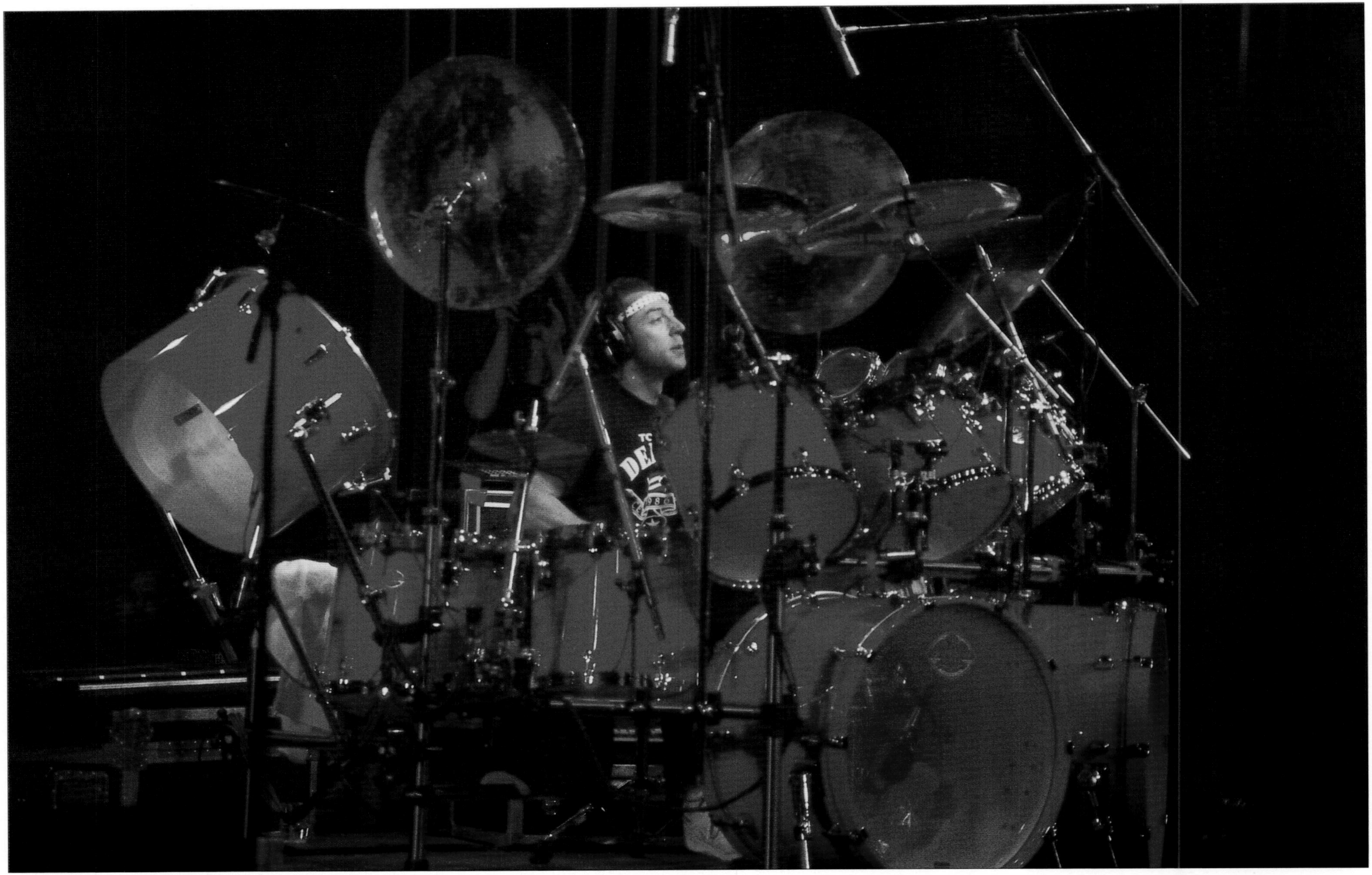

Simon Phillips

Charlie Watts

Tony Williams

Dennis Chambers

Photo by the Author

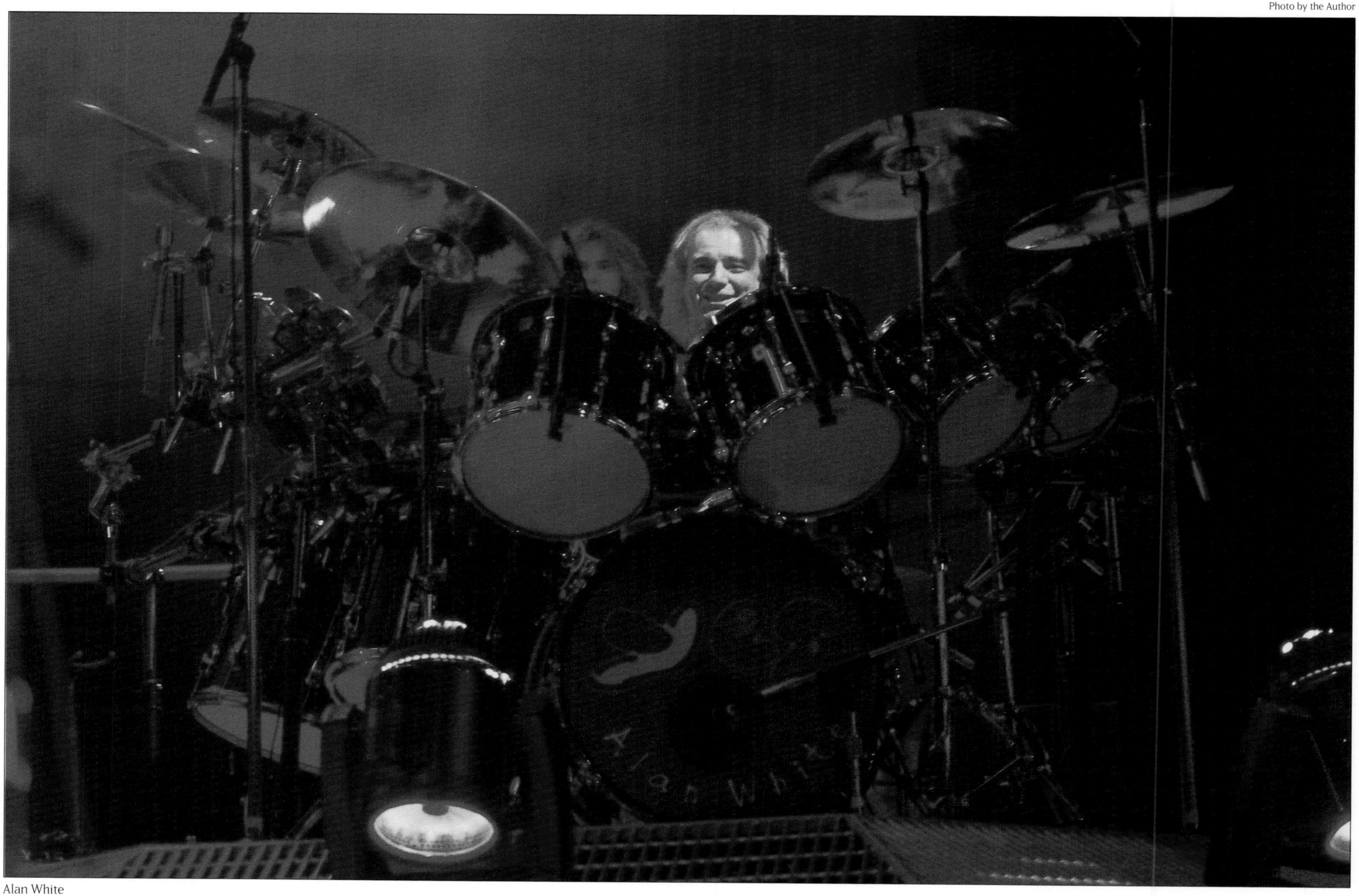

Alan White

Mitch Mitchell

Airto Moreira

Mickey Hart and Bill Kreutzmann

Chad Smith

Neil Peart

Once upon a time there was a band out of Los Angeles called the Doors. Their songs, set against a blues and jazz backdrop, were sharp reflections of the turbulent state of affairs in 1960s America. The band became a symbol of rebellion to young Americans, stretching the boundaries of popular songwriting, provoking controversy among the establishment, and making some very good music along the way. John Densmore, drummer for the Doors, got to see it all from behind his Ludwig drums.

Densmore's style was influenced by the playing of jazz drummers like Elvin Jones and Art Blakey. Growing up a drummer in L.A. in the sixties meant playing every kind of music for every occasion. "I had to play waltzes, fox trots, cha-cha-chas, so that was really good for me," he told writer Robyn Flans. After playing with future Doors guitarist Robbie Krieger in a couple of bands, Densmore met organist Ray

In concert with the Mod Orange Ludwigs.

Manzarek and formed the Doors with Manzarek's two brothers and a shy singer-songwriter named Jim Morrison. Robbie Krieger came into the fold after Manzarek's brothers quit, cementing the final lineup of the Doors.

Although the spotlight often shone brightest on the magnetic personality of Jim Morrison, Densmore and the other Doors played an equal part in constructing the classic jams that the band became known for. The writing of songs like "Light My Fire," "The End," and "Hello, I Love You" was a collaborative effort. "Everybody had equal input," Densmore told Flans, "and if anybody was dissatisfied about anything, he said so." The song structures were elastic, lending themselves to open-ended live improvisation. Densmore's jazz influences are clearly stated on songs like "Riders On the Storm" and "L.A. Woman," with its dynamic interplay between guitar, organ, and drums.

On blues tunes, Densmore said he would tune his drums to the I, IV, and V chords of the song he was recording to be more melodic with the rest of the band. He also favored using worn drum heads to achieve the sounds he wanted. "I hated new skins and new drums," he said. "I liked to beat them up until they started barking back at me."

Densmore played Gretsch drums on the early Doors records, then switched to Ludwig. He had a Mod Orange pearl set at the height of the sixties psychedelic craze. His snare drum was the ever-present 5" Supra-phonic 400. "I had a Ludwig snare all the way and still have my Ludwig snare," he told *Modern Drummer*. "I still have the original Doors one. I still love the sound."

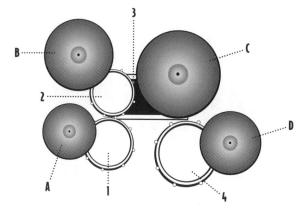

John Densmore's Kit Circa 1969...Ludwig drums, Mod Orange Pearl, w/Zildjian cymbals

1... 5 x 14" Supra-phonic Snare Drum
2... 9 x 13" Tom-Tom
3... 22" Bass Drum
4... 16 x 16" Floor Tom

A... 14" Hi-hats
B... 18" Crash
C... 20" or 22" Riveted Ride
D... 16" Crash

With the Jimi Hendrix Experience in the late sixties.

Michael Ochs Archives

It's a safe bet to say the world may never see another guitarist as originally brilliant as Jimi Hendrix. What Buddy Rich was to the drums, Hendrix was to the guitar. His playing transcended any labels, drawing as much from John Coltrane as Elmore James, floating through blues and jazz changes quicker than a hot knife through butter. The musicians that played with Hendrix were required to fly in the eye of the storm, twisting and turning with him on his wild excursions of genius. Most drummers would have sold their soul to play with him. Mitch Mitchell was lucky enough to be chosen for the task.

Mitchell was a young session drummer in London, with a few good name gigs under his belt, when he was approached to play with Hendrix on a short tour in France. Mitchell's jazz-inflected drumming turned out to be the perfect counterpoint to Hendrix's guitar playing, and the Jimi Hendrix Experience was born. With Noel Redding on bass, the three musicians went on to conquer the rock world, playing the Monterey Pop Festival in 1967 as relative unknowns.

After Monterey and a short tour as the warm-up act for the Monkees, Hendrix's star began to rise quickly. With the albums *Are You Experienced*, *Axis: Bold as Love*, and *Electric Ladyland*, Mitchell created a close relationship with Hendrix that was honed over the many live shows the band did together. "I always felt completely at home with Jimi," writes Mitchell in his wonderful memoirs, *Jimi Hendrix: Inside the Experience*. "The two of us working together—it was so easy." Listen to "Manic Depression" and "If Six Was Nine" to hear how much Hendrix relied on Mitchell to really push the song. Mitchell quotes freely from Elvin Jones and Art Blakey, playing around and within the beat. When asked about his onstage improvisations with the Experience, Hendrix was quoted as saying, "The drums make it happen."

The drums that made it happen for Mitchell in the early Hendrix days were a five-piece Premier kit. In 1967, he got a Silver Sparkle Ludwig set, with two floor toms, à la Buddy Rich. He played different variations of that setup, going to a natural maple kit over time. "To me," Mitchell told *Modern Drummer*, "the impressive thing is seeing, say, Elvin or Tony and saying 'how the hell are they getting that much sound and tone from such small drums, and so few drums?' "

Mitch playing in a French TV Studio, 1967.

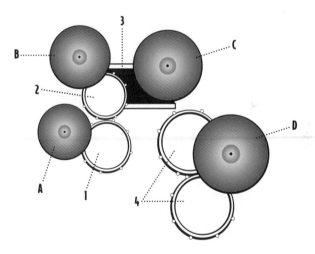

Mitch Mitchell's Kit Circa 1967...Ludwig drums, Silver Sparkle, w/Zildjian cymbals

1... 5 x 14" Supra-phonic Snare Drum
2... 9 x 13" Tom-Tom
3... 22" or 24" Bass Drum
4... 2- 16 x 16" Floor Toms

A... 14" Hi-hats
B... 16" Crash
C... 18" Crash Ride
D... 20" Riveted Ride

The funkiest man in showbiz.

Courtesy Clyde Stubblefield

Clyde Stubblefield remembers feeling the rhythm very early on. "In my hometown of Chattanooga, Tennessee", he recalls, "there was a factory, had a big tall smokestack with compressed air coming out of it. We lived in a valley, and that sound would echo off the mountains giving a 1+ beat, like a metronome, waking me up around 8:00 in the morning. The old washing machines made a sound going back and forth all the time. Whistling tea kettles, tick-tock clocks, all that got me so grooved up, I just started playing the drums, I couldn't take it no more."

Stubblefield played his syncopated Southern funk for some of James Brown's finest records in the 1960s. From "Cold Sweat" and "Say It Loud (I'm Black and I'm Proud)" to "Mother Popcorn," he laid the foundation for the ground-breaking grooves that started a revolution in soul music. "When I first started with Brown, he had five drummers and I was the sixth one. There were six sets of drums sitting on the stage. He had special drummers for everything, one guy playing one type of groove and such. Then he fired everybody except me and Jabo [John Starks]. He called on Jabo for certain ballads and things and called on me for the hard, ass-kicking shit." Writes the Godfather, James Brown, in his autobiography: "Starks and Clyde Stubblefield were two of the funkiest drummers you could find. They did it to death."

In the driver's seat with the Clyde Stubblefield Band.

Brown's method of recording was collaborative, says Stubblefield. "Somebody would come in with a riff or a bass line, and then everybody would get behind their instruments and run it down. Then they'd say, 'Okay, we got the groove, let's put a bridge or a break here.' After you got the groove, then you'd start to form it."

Stubblefield firmly cemented his place in drum history in 1969, when he went into a Cincinnati studio with Brown to record a number based on a drum beat he had come up with. The song, appropriately titled "Funky Drummer," features an improvised eight-bar drum break that became the standard against which all funk drumming would be measured. The groove was so undeniably soulful that 20 years later it became a favorite of producers, who digitally sampled it for the foundation of dance and rap songs. Clyde has heard his famous beat sampled and looped on songs by Madonna, Public Enemy, and Sinead O'Connor. "I love it. The only thing I don't like is they never acknowledge it or say thank you. I think that's disrespect. But I'm still honored that they used it."

Brown signed an endorsement contract with the Vox company in the late sixties, giving the members of his band Vox drums, guitars, and amps. "We experimented with those Vox drums for a while. I couldn't take the snare drums. They had no sound, no vibration, so I would always use my Ludwig or Slingerland snare drums. After Vox, I went back to playing Ludwig. Now I endorse Remo drums and Sabian cymbals. I love them."

His trademark snare drum patterns are noticeable for their tight, crisp sound. "Live, I try to tune my drums like I'm sitting in the recording studio listening to them on headphones. I don't know if I tune them high or low, but when they get to the sound I want, that's when I stop."

Recording, producing, and playing with his own band keeps Clyde very busy these days. He released a CD of grooves that can be sampled by a whole new generation of funksters. He tries not to get too analytical when it comes to his drumming. "It's just stuff that comes off the top of your head. I never read music. Whatever the groove calls for, I just feel it."

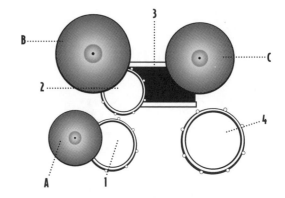

Clyde Stubblefield's Kit Circa 1969...Ludwig drums, Silver or Red Sparkle, w/Zildjian cymbals

1... 5 x 14" Chrome Supra-phonic 400 Snare Drum
2... 9 x 13" Tom-Tom
3... 22" Bass Drum

4... 16 x 16" Floor Tom
A... 14" Hi-hats
B... 20" Ride
C... 18" Crash

Bernard with his band in the early 1970s.

Call it what you want, Bernard Purdie has his own name for the fat-pocket groove he has provided for so many great songs over the last 30 years. "I call it my 'loco-motion'. It's a feel and a very positive attitude, but it also means being simple, giving folks what they want, which is time."

The time Purdie plays has been an essential part of some very important music. His work with Aretha Franklin, King Curtis, James Brown, Steely Dan, and countless others is testimony to his great flexibility. Like any great session player, he is hired for his capacity to produce magic out of the little black notes on a chart. Listen to the way he kicks into the bridge on Steely Dan's "Home at Last," making rhythmic sense of a very complex structure of jazz changes, staying tight and supremely funky. "The dominant factor for me is to play what people feel, what they like, which is the backbeat. I try to capture the rhythm of any style of song that I'm playing."

Backbeat is what Purdie is all about. It was his love of rhythm that made him start playing drums at age three. "My first money gig, I think I was twelve. I got paid eight dollars. That was good money then. I was playing hillbilly and country music, which was big at the time. I was a country boy from Maryland.

"I always looked over the shoulders of the players. I used to watch horn players and I found that the licks they were doing was something I could do on the drums."

One of the great Purdie drum parts is the classic groove he played on Aretha Franklin's "Rock Steady." The tune finds the "Pretty One" doing what he does best: driving the band. He supports Chuck Rainey's bass line in a style that suggests a reggae feel with some southern-fried soul thrown in. "I had just come back from Jamaica and I was teaching the feeling and attitudes to everybody in the band. Chuck Rainey, Cornell Dupree, Donny Hathaway, they were all there. It was new to them and we really created a different thing. You see, each feel, eighth note, dotted, triplet, has a mind of its own. I just try to help to make sure the attitude is gonna be right.

"Everybody laughs at me when I tell them that when Aretha sings, she's singing for me. When I play, I'm playing just for her. It's a

Mr. Rock Steady behind his Sonor Drums.

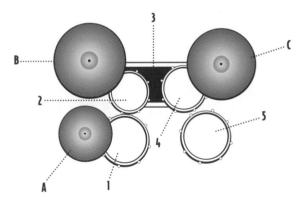

Bernard Purdie's Kit Circa 1969...Sonor drums w/Avedis Zildjian cymbals

1... 5 x 14" Snare Drum
2... 8 x 12" Tom-Tom
3... 18" Bass Drum
4... 9 x 13" Tom-Tom
5... 14 x 14" Floor Tom
A... 14" New Beat Hi-hats
B... 19" Medium Thin Crash Ride
C... 18" Mini-cup Ride

What the well-dressed drummer is playing.

mutual understanding and feeling. That's how we communicate.

"James Brown was different. His demands were to be on time and keep the time going. Very few solos. You had to keep an eye out for cues. When we did things live, I had to watch his feet and his butt."

Purdie credits producer/engineers Tom Dowd and Gene Paul for the drum sound he got on all those great sessions for Atlantic records. "They could really make those drums sound good in the studio. Most of the time I was using Sonor [drums]. I also had a Ludwig metal snare at that time. I had a Gretsch snare and I had an old Wolf snare drum from 1933 and that snare drum is one I used on a great deal of records. It wasn't a normal size, it was like 6$\frac{3}{8}$" [deep]. I was also using an 18" bass drum."

Along with the bass drum, Purdie played 12" and 13" mounted toms, a 14" floor tom, and Zildjian cymbals. He still uses Sonor drums and now endorses Sabian cymbals.

While times often change demand for a musician's services, Purdie still enjoys a busy schedule of playing. He releases jazz records with his band the 3B's, makes instructional videos for drummers, records grooves for a CD to be used for sampling and dance music, and still tours with Aretha Franklin.

Attitude is a word that comes up often in conversation with Bernard. He feels that a good attitude is a the key to making good music. "Allow everybody to do their thing, but at the same time, you can control the feel. Each song I've played on represents a piece of me."

Tim Motion

Jack DeJohnette

1970s... The Beat Goes On

Ian Dickson

Carmine Appice

The greatest revolutions in music are always born as a reaction to the times and a mixing of styles and influences. The Miles Davis bands of the late 1960s and early 1970s were breeding grounds for young musicians keen on expanding the framework of jazz by incorporating rock, funk, and avant-garde influences. Out of these groups came the first generation of electric jazz composers and players, people like Herbie Hancock, Wayne Shorter, Chick Corea, and Joe Zawinul. Drummers Tony Williams, Jack DeJohnette, and Billy Cobham cut their teeth in Davis' band and went on to become some of the most dominant artists in their field, altering the musical landscape as leaders or co-leaders of their own groups.

The outrageous jams of fusion bands like Mahavishnu Orchestra gave impetus to fuel a crossbreeding of styles on the rock scene. The songs of Yes, Emerson, Lake, and Palmer, Genesis, and King Crimson reflected a recognition of classical music as a valid ingredient to add to the stew. The hard riff-based rock of Led Zeppelin, Deep Purple, and Black Sabbath also relied on a drum-heavy bedrock to get their point across. The late-seventies response to heavy instrumental rock was punk and new wave, which produced another batch of excellent players like Stewart Copeland, Topper Headon, Clem Burke, and Pete Thomas.

The classic four-piece drum set was eclipsed by bigger kits with deeper drums and more cymbals. Recording

Collection of the Author

Staccato Drums

ALICE COOPER
DRUMMER
NEAL SMITH
Total SLINGERLAND

Frank Driggs Collection

Neal Smith

Slingerland Ad

Premier Ad

Rogers Roy Burns Ad

engineers and producers became more dominant in dictating what drums sounded like. Bottom heads were taken off tom-toms and bass drums to get a louder, deeper sound. Like the American auto industry of the seventies, the "Big Four" drum companies Ludwig, Slingerland, Gretsch, and Rogers lost ground to the new Japanese import drums of Yamaha, Pearl, and Tama. To confuse matters more, the traditional drum kit and drummer now had to compete with the advent of drum machines and samplers.

An interesting thing began to happen in the 1980s. Perhaps as a result of the onslaught of electronics and glut of low-quality instruments on the market, drummers began to collect and play the

Ludwig Ad

Nigel Olsson

drums of the past. Radio Kings, Black Beauties, and Gretsch-Gladstones fell back into favor in recording studios and on concert stages. Tube lugs and single-ply shells, previously dismissed as old-fashioned and impractical, were again showing up on top-shelf drum sets. Many companies, aware of the yearning for simple craftsmanship, began releasing their versions of the old classics. In 1994 Ludwig reissued an exact replica of Ringo Starr's Oyster Black drum set, calling it "The Fab 4-piece," while a reborn Slingerland planned to bring back the legendary Radio King.

The logical conclusion of all the advances in the art of drumming are evident. Drummers finally seem to have accepted and even welcomed the new electronic digital technology. They mix the old and the new to create hybrid and innovative instruments, taking their sounds and rhythms into the twenty-first century. The beat goes on...

Tama Ad

Courtesy Zildjian Co.

Dennis St. John
Drummer with
NEIL DIAMOND
plays the
ALL AMERICAN OUTFIT

Dennis St. John

The drum kit that ate London, Moon onstage, 1974.

Ian Dickson

He wasn't exactly Mr. Subtlety on the drum kit. No light brush work for him, thank you very much. He painted in broad strokes, beating out a roaring wall of drums to fit Pete Townshend's manic guitar, John Entwistle's regal bass, and Roger Daltrey's gritty vocals. Sadly, the music world will never see Keith Moon's equal. He was a complex mix of genius and lunatic, tremendously exciting to watch and hear, always playing with great energy and flair. The music he recorded with the Who still stands as an example of some of the greatest rock drumming ever.

Moon more than made up for his lack of technical virtuosity with an abundance of raw energy and inherent showmanship. He credited Gene Krupa as inspiration for his onstage stick twirling and outrageous tom fills. All the attention that was focused on Moon's notorious offstage adventures (the time he drove a rented Cadillac into a hotel swimming pool, for instance) subtracts from the true dynamic ability and originality he brought to the drum set. From the early Who classics like "My Generation" and "The Kids Are Alright" to "Bargain" and "I'm One" from later albums, Moon came up with distinctive drum parts that added drive and

An early shot of the red sparkle Premier kit.

urgency to the material. *Live at Leeds*, from 1970, is a spectacular document of the Who's stage show, with Moon tearing the roof off the house on "Summertime Blues."

Although Moon probably wrecked more kits than most of us will ever own, he was careful in choosing the appearance of his drums to fit his jaunty image. He played Ludwig before going over to Premier, who supplied him with an endless selection of drums, including the infamous "Pictures of Lily" kit, complete with dancing go-go girls and pop art painted on the shells. At the time of his death, Moon was considering an endorsement of the horn-shaped drums made by Staccato. "Certainly Keith was about to go with Staccato," remarks Bob Henrit, Kinks drummer and a friend of Moon's. "It would have been a much more flamboyant kit for him anyway. It fit his image perfectly."

Moon didn't talk much about his choice of drums, but Henrit remembers him using a Ludwig Supra-phonic 400 snare and a wood-shell Gretsch as well as the metal-shell snare drums Premier provided. Henrit recalls an episode that reflects Moon's matter-of-fact attitude towards drum equipment. "One day, he turned up at my drum shop in the Rolls Royce with a whole boot full of snare drums. He said 'Dear boy, I don't need these anymore, would you like to take them?' "

Wrecking their equipment became one of the Who's trademarks. In the early days, they literally went into deep debt with instrument bills. Because of his raucous behavior behind the kit, special reinforcement was added to Moon's Premiers to prolong their life. Rogers Swiv-o-matic mounts were attached to the tom-toms to strengthen the drums. A connecting device was used to keep his double bass drums in line as well.

Over the years, Moon's kit got bigger and bigger, eventually numbering up to 16 drums. The idea was to have a drum anywhere his flailing arms could reach, assuring even crazier tom-tom fills and cymbal crashes. On the 1973 album *Quadrophenia*, arguably Moons finest work, he plays layers upon layers of drums, heroically pushing songs like "Drowned" and "5:15" to the crazy extreme. There's no way to ignore the extravagant brilliance of his drumming on the epic double album, and that's just the way Keith would have wanted it.

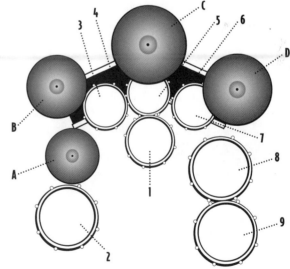

Keith Moon's Kit Circa 1966 ...Premier drums, Red Sparkle, w/Paiste and Zildjian cymbals

1... 5 x 14" Ludwig Supra-phonic 400 Snare Drum
2... 16 x 16" Floor Tom
3... 8 x 14" Tom-Tom
4... 22" Bass Drum
5... 8 x 14" Tom-Tom
6... 22" Bass Drum

7... 8 x 14" Tom-Tom
8... 16 x 16" Floor Tom
9... 16 x 16" Floor Tom
A... 14 or 15" Hi-hats
B... 16" Crash
C... 20" Crash or Ride
D... 18" Crash

The hammer of the gods onstage with Led Zeppelin.

Jim Cummins/Star File

Although some drummers have made a career out of trying to sound like the late, great John Bonham, none have ever succeeded. Bonham was a one-of-a-kind original, a working-class drummer from England's Black Country, big as a house and strong as a bull. So solid was his groove, and so huge his sound, he became the benchmark by which all other hard rock drummers are measured. When he stomped out a beat for Led Zeppelin, the earth would shake and rattle.

Bonham worked closely with guitarist Jimmy Page to create the riff-heavy songs that became Zeppelin's trademark. While most rock drummers use the bass line to dictate the beat they play, Bonham would follow Page's guitar to intensify the groove. On songs like "Custard Pie," "Out on the Tiles," "The Ocean," and "When the Levee Breaks," Bonham's drums are a percussive mirror of Page's rhythm playing, strongly stating his case with power and swing.

Vistalites and Tympani, Keezar Stadium, 1974.

One of Bonham's most enduring legacies is the huge drum sound he had, both live and on record. He used Ludwig drums, including a 6.5"-deep Supra-phonic snare drum, 18" and 20" floor toms, and a big 12 x 15" tom-tom mounted over a 14 x 26" bass drum, usually with little muffling and no holes cut in the front head. He tensioned his drums fairly tight, especially the snare and bass drum to get a big, resonant sound. The tremendous power in his legs and hands transferred to a great attack on the drums and cymbals. Drum tech Jeff Ochletree worked with Led Zeppelin for two tours in the 1970s and got to see Bonham work both onstage and in the studio.

"The reasons those drums sounded so good was performance, good mike placement, and recording in very live rooms," he says. "They would record in studios with high ceilings, wood floors, and lots of reflective surfaces."

Engineer Eddie Kramer, who often recorded Bonham in the studio, wisely chose to let Bonham's drums speak for themselves. He used ambient microphone placement instead of close miking, to get a natural, unprocessed sound from the kit. Bonham took great joy in playing drums that sounded like drums, with all the sustain and ring out in the open for the whole world to hear. When he used muffling, it was only the slightest amount, and always in the bass drum. "A couple kick drums had nothing in them, but one of them had cut up newspaper in it for muffling," recalls Ochletree. "One day I changed the heads and forgot to put the newspaper back in. Bonham says to me, 'The bass drum sounds good, it's bellowing.' I told him I forgot to put the paper back in. He gave me the evil eye and said, 'Starting to take the law into your own hands, eh?'"

For all the analysis that has been aimed at his drum sound, one fact is often overlooked: John Bonham knew how to hit a drum. His playing could be extremely heavy, yet he had a light swinging touch that can be best heard on tunes like "The Rain Song." He was influenced by the work of soul and funk drummers Zigaboo Modeliste, Benny Benjamin, Clyde Stubblefield, and Al Jackson Jr. He enjoyed nothing better than to sit back and groove. "I don't play what I don't like," he told *Melody Maker* in a rare interview. "I'm a simple, straight-ahead drummer and I don't try to be anything better than I am."

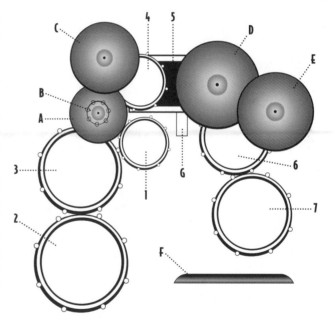

John Bonham's Kit Circa 1976...Ludwig drums* w/Paiste cymbals

1... 6½ x 14" Supra-phonic 400 Snare Drum	**A...** 15" Sound Edge Hi-hats
2... 26" Tympany	**B...** Ching ring
3... 24" Tympany	**C...** 18 or 20" Medium Crash
4... 12 x 15" Tom-Tom	**D...** 22 or 24" Medium Ride
5... 26" Bass Drum	**E...** 20" Medium Crash
6... 18 x 18" Floor Tom	**F...** 36" Paiste Gong
7... 20 x 20" Floor Tom	**G...** Speed King Pedal

*Bonham used different kits during this period, including green sparkle, silver sparkle, Amber Vistalite, and stainless steel. He used both black dot and Remo Emperor heads.

Laying down the law with the Stones.

Ian Dickson

It's not state-of-the-art drumming. It's certainly not ripping solos, twirling sticks, or flashy theatrics. It *is* style and swing. He is Charlie Watts, drummer for "The Greatest Rock and Roll Band in the World," the Rolling Stones. For more than 30 years, Watts has played his laid-back beat behind the Stones' guitar-fueled rhythms. He has the ability to both propel and support a song, finding just the right balance of drive and groove. His playing is so loose and honest it sometimes sounds as if it teeters on the edge of breaking up, something Jim Keltner once described as "desperate sounding, but relaxed at the same time."

Watts had a reputation as one of London's better drummers when he joined the Rolling Stones in 1962. Previous to the Stones, he had played in Alexis Korner's Blues Incorporated, a band he says he left because he felt he wasn't good enough. The drummer who replaced him was none other than Ginger Baker.

The Stones defined the image of bad-boy rock and roll with songs like "Street Fighting Man," "Under My Thumb," "Honky-Tonk Women," and "Bitch" in the sixties and seventies. Although the band earned a reputation as outlaws, Watts remained the stoic observer behind his drums, staying quiet and dignified. Through the eighties, and into the nineties, Charlie's beat has never wavered. He remains as consistent and economical in his playing as ever. In 1985 he formed the Charlie Watts Big Band, getting a chance to return to his roots and fulfill a lifelong passion for jazz.

It was his affection for the jazz of the forties and fifties that shaped Charlie's choice of equipment. He owns a few Gretsch kits, including a classic green sparkle jazz set from the 1950s and a black nitron set from the sixties. In the sixties he played a sky-blue pearl Ludwig kit with the ubiquitous Supra-phonic 400 snare drum. His main drum set now is a late-fifties Gretsch in natural maple with 12" and 16" tom-toms and a 22" bass drum. He plays a 6.5" Supra-phonic that was appropriated from S.I.R. rehearsal studios in New York. The famous trashy-sounding cymbal that is heard on some of the later Stones recordings is an 18" UFIP china. Charlie also uses an old pair of 14" Zildjian hi-hats, a 16" Zildjian crash, and a no-name 18" flat ride.

To see Watts play is to gain a lesson in powerful understatement. He is a groove player who throws in odd fills and offbeat snare hits at just the right time, making his presence known and felt, but always with the greatest of taste.

Playing the backbeat on his vintage Gretsches.

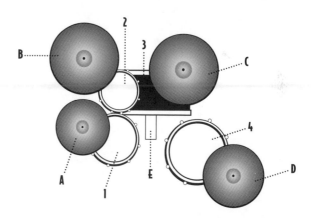

Charlie Watts' Kit 1994...Gretsch drums, Maple Finish, Late 1950s Vintage, w/Zildjian cymbals

1... 6½ x 14" Ludwig Supra-phonic 400 Snare Drum, 1970s Vintage	**A...** 14" Hi-hats
	B... 18" UFIP China
2... 8 x 12" Tom-Tom	**C...** 18" Flat Ride
3... 22" Bass Drum	**D...** 16" or 18" Crash
4... 16 x 16" Floor Tom	**E...** WFL Speed King Pedal

Other equipment includes: Rogers Swiv-o-matic hi-hat stand, Gretsch cymbal stands, and a Buck Rogers snare drum stand.

Jim Keltner, 1994.

Jim Keltner is a soul drummer in the best sense of the word. What you hear on record comes straight up through the sticks via his heart. His loose, funky style is sly, hip, and invariably off the cuff. He never approaches a song or fill the same way twice. "I started out with pretty good technique," Keltner says, "but I just found myself fighting it all the time doing studio work. I read in articles where people talk about my style being identifiable. I just don't see that. I see an absence of style because of the studio thing."

The studio thing is where Jim and his drumming have made the greatest impact. The list of artists who have called on his talents reads like a Who's Who of popular music: Bob Dylan, John Lennon, Ry Cooder, Eric Clapton, Pink Floyd, Neil Young, Elvis Costello, Jackson Brown, Randy Newman, Joe Cocker, and the Traveling Wilburys. He has also had the opportunity to record and tour with Ringo Starr, a drummer whose work he admires a great deal.

Keltner didn't reach the top overnight. It took plenty of short money gigs and demo sessions to get his name around Los Angeles. When he was first starting out in the studios in the

Courtesy Jim Keltner

Jimmie Lee Keltner rides the rocket to stardom.

sixties, his role model was Hal Blaine. "When I heard Hal play for the first time, that's when I realized there was a sound I wanted to get. His bass drum and snare drum just were so nice. It was calf heads on the bass drum, so I did the same thing. So did Jimmy Gordon. Once I had kind of gotten Hal down, and was copying him for so long, I gravitated toward Jimmy, who was also a Hal disciple.

"I was influenced heavily by the New Orleans thing, but I don't know if that's my style. I listened to Levon [Helm] for so long. I always tried to cop that feel, but I never really could get it. He was such a funny-type player. He didn't have any technique, he had to make up for it in this great awkward way, it just sounded incredible. He's the reason why I've tried to undo my technique all these years.

"Hopefully it would be a short time that you emulate people whose sound you like and then you move on and get something of your own. I don't know if that ever happens though. I still find myself listening to all kinds of people for inspiration."

In a business that encourages conformity of sound and style, Keltner is an individualist who steers clear of trends. When it comes to equipment he is as likely to use a pair of 16" hi-hats as he is a pair of 14". He also has a sizable bevy of snare drums at his disposal to use as he sees fit. "Generally I play a regular kit. If it needs some strange thing, I've got a rack to hang things around the drum kit. I use all DW drums except for the occasional vintage snare drum, and I also use snare drums made by Ross Garfield. I've never liked many snare drums over 6" deep. I usually use a 5" or 5.5". For a long time I used a 4", but that became so popular that the sound was

overused. I tend to go away from whatever the current sound is, it's just something automatic. My favorite vintage snare drum is an old Super Sensitive with the double snares in a faded green pearl. I've had it since the mid seventies. I use it all the time. It's not a slamming drum or a big backbeat drum. I use it when I want something to be unique—real sensitive, but fat.

"I generally use a 12" rack and 16" floor or a 10" and 12" rack with the 16" floor tom. The depths vary. DW is so into different depths and plies, I can't keep up with it.

"I like the difference between a 12 and 16" [tom-tom]. When you start getting a 12" and 14" to me there's not that much of a difference, you get into tuning the drums to a scale, which I'm not a fan of. You have to be a very articulate player if you're gonna do that. Jeff Porcaro did it in a beautiful way. He played so articulately that he pulled it off.

"I saw Al Jackson play in a studio in L.A. and I was waiting for the magical drum set, but he used a rental kit and made them sound amazing, just pure music. It's totally the way he played it. It's in the way you play the melody on the drums that counts."

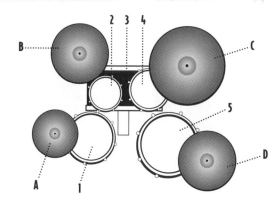

Jim Keltner's Kit Autumn 1994...DW drums w/Paiste cymbals—complete line*

1... 5½ x 14" Snare Drum**
2... 10" Tom-Tom, optional
3... 16 x 18", 16 x 20", 14 x 22", 12 x 24", or
14 x 24" Bass Drum
4... 12" Tom-Tom, variable depths

5... 16 x 16" Floor Tom
A... 12, 14, 15, 16, or 18" Hi-hats
B... 15 or 20" Crash
C... 20, 21, or 22" Ride
D... 15, 16, 17, 20, 21, or 22" Crash

*Note: Jim will mix and match drums and cymbals according to the requirements of the session. This diagram is to give an idea of what a typical setup might be.
**DW Solid shell, Edge or Brass. Also a Garfield custom and assorted vintage snares.

Even too quick for the camera.

Not only is he in possession of some of the most jaw-dropping, eye-popping chops ever unleashed on the drum set, but Dennis Chambers can work a simple 2 and 4 backbeat like nobody's business. Whether he is supplying the pulse for the big band rump shake of the P-Funk All Stars, playing neo-bop with guitarist John McLaughlin and organist Joey DeFrancesco, or driving Steely Dan's road show, Dennis is always on top of the gig, making sure the music is grooving and moving.

Growing up in Baltimore, Dennis absorbed a lot of different musical influences. "I listened to everybody that was out there," he recalls. "From King records and Stax and Motown, to all the jazz guys: Tony, Art Blakey, Elvin, Buddy Rich, everybody."

Photographic proof that Dennis only has two arms and two legs.

In the bright light of his outlandish technique, it's often easy to forget what a tasteful, musical drummer Chambers really is. He sounds comfortable in almost any situation, tailoring his playing to support the needs of the music. He also makes sure he chooses the right drums for the gig. "It all depends on the music," he says about his setup. "If I'm playing bop, I don't need a big boomy bass drum and power toms. It wouldn't be right for the music. Like the stuff with John [McLaughlin], I'm using a 20" bass drum and regular-sized toms. I have the drums [tuned] up real high."

Dennis' first big gig was touring with George Clinton and crew in Parliament-Funkadelic's crazy live revue. He had the job of kicking the 20-piece band through a four-hour set. "When I was with P-Funk, it was a pretty big band, so I had a 24" bass drum with three rack and two floor toms. I used to have to play stick percussion too, so there were a lot of things going on."

After the P-Funk gig, Dennis spent time in Special FX and John Scofield's band, then moved on to lend his talents to many different projects. His facility just seems to get better and better with each new assignment. His approach to the drums is always inventive and risky, playing fast bass and snare drum patterns and blinding tom-tom fills. His sound remains an important part of his identity. He plays Pearl Master Series drums, which he says "sound really good. They're warm and deep sounding. I really like them.

"I'm using a lot of different snare drums. I have a Firchie drum, and a snare from Baltimore Drums. I like the warmth of a wood drum. But I use metal drums for different things too." He owns a vintage Ludwig Black Beauty snare drum that doesn't leave the house. "I have another Black Beauty from the sixties that I used to use with P-Funk."

Dennis relies on his ears for tuning his tom-toms. "I don't tune to a note. I tighten them to what I like to hear. I tune them in thirds from wherever the snare drum pitch is. The top [heads] are usually tighter than the bottoms on the racks, but it's the opposite on the floor, because I want the floor toms to sound big and warm. But again, it all depends on the music, for what I'm going after."

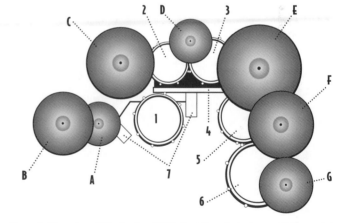

Dennis Chambers' Kit Spring 1994...Pearl Master Series drums w/Zildjian cymbals

1... 6½ x 14" Snare Drum	A... 12" S.R. Hi-hats
2... 8 x 12" Tom-Tom	B... 16" A Custom
3... 9 x 13" Tom-Tom	C... 18" A Custom
4... 20" Bass Drum	D... 12" K Dark Splash
5... 14 x 14" Floor Tom	E... 22" K Custom Ride
6... 16 x 16" Floor Tom	F... 17" A Custom Crash
7... DW Turbo Accelerator Double Bass Drum Pedal	G... 14" China Oriental

Airto and his table of percussion.

Photo by the Author

Photo montage by the Author

Airto Moreira's Kit 1994...Eames drums w/Zildjian cymbals

1... 6½ x 14" Snare Drum
2... 6 x 12" Tom-Tom
3... 6½ x 13" Tom-Tom
4... 12 x 16" Floor Tom
5... 20" Bass Drum
6... Piece of Cardboard Box
A... 13" K Z Hi-hats
B... 16" K Crash
C... 20" Flat Ride
D... Woodblocks
E... 8" Chinese Cymbal
F... Englehart Crasher
G... Chinese Wooden Toys
H... Portuguese Wooden Shoes
J... Wooden Bird Call
K... Englehart Octagonal Metal Tambourine

L... Bell Chimes
M...8" Chinese Gong
N... Noise Maker
O... Caxixis from Africa & Brazil
P... Wooden Board with Wire
Q... Refrigerator Hose
R... Japanese Instrument used in Kabuki Theater
S... 26" Chinese Cymbal
T... Brazilian Noise Maker
U... Tambourim
V... 10" Chinese Gong
W... 12" Chinese Gong
X... 3 Cowbells
Y... Chinese Gong

Note: Airto uses a double bass drum pedal and a remote hi-hat pedal. On any given night he has a large array of percussion instruments to choose from.

I was probably six years old when I went to this show in a park in the little town in South Brazil where I grew up," remembers Airto Moreira. "Everybody was standing up, and I was too small to see, so my father set me up on his shoulder. These people walk on stage and they start playing this incredible music. This guy was singing and playing the *sanfona* [a type of accordion] and he had a beautiful hat on. There was a woman playing percussion with this drum, a *zabumba*, and she was playing a shaker in her left hand. I was very impressed. I felt a great desire to do that. It was like a voice saying, 'If you want, you can do that.' I looked around and the people were so happy. I couldn't believe everybody was feeling the same thing. It really made a mark in my soul. I think that triggered the percussionist in me."

Airto has shared his love of percussive sounds with the world for most of his life. He played in Brazil with Quarteto Novo, a group he fondly remembers as "the best band I ever had." He came to the United States in the 1960s and played both drum set and percussion in many different settings with Cannonball Adderley, Chick Corea (in the first incarnation of Return to Forever), Weather Report, and Miles Davis. It was with Davis that his arsenal of percussion really grew.

"When I was playing with Miles Davis, I used to put my instruments on the floor around me. I had a lot of small stuff. Then Miles said, 'I'll give you money and you go there [Brazil] and get a lot of shit.' I went to Brazil and bought three trunks full of stuff. Then I needed more room, and things just started growing. Then, when I played with Weather Report I used two small tables and some things to hang stuff, so things grew a little more."

He was still playing either drums or hand percussion, but not both at the same time. The problem, as Airto saw it, was how to incorporate the drum kit with his table of percussion. The music he was playing with his wife, singer and musician Flora Purim, called for both. "With our band, we had a problem: we always had to call a percussionist or a drummer to do what I couldn't do. Peter Englehart had made me a percussion table, but I hadn't thought about putting a bass drum under it. At that time I had congas on my left and timbales on my right. When you play congas, that's it; you can't do anything else, so I got rid of the congas."

Airto included a bass drum and floor tom to the percussion table to add new dimensions to his music, but he still wanted the range of sound that only a full drum set could provide. "One day I was playing in Boston, and Joe MacSweeney from Eames Drums came over and said he was gonna make a snare for me. And then I talked to him about building a special drum set that would be light to carry. So Joe built it for me. It's got a beautiful sound. It's not too loud and not too wimpy."

The kit MacSweeney built for Airto includes three single-headed tom-toms and a bass drum, which all pack inside one another for easy transporting.

Airto placed the bass drum underneath his table and set the rest of the kit up on his left. He uses a double pedal to access the bass drum from the drum set. He also uses a remote hi-hat pedal, which allows him to straddle his floor tom instead of his snare drum. "This way, when I want to play drums, I sit down on my high seat and I can play, but at the same time I can reach my percussion. Now I can play both things at the same time."

Airto keeps a wide assortment of percussive goodies on his table, including an old refrigerator hose, bird and game calls, Portuguese

Striking one of his many cymbals.

wooden shoes, cymbals, bells, and blocks of every sort, and the custom metal crashers and tambourines made by Pete Englehart. He likes to mix different sounds to create a response in his listeners.

"If you do something good with the music, then people feel real good and they want to give you something back. They don't just applaud and say how great you are, they want to give you a part of themselves to mix with your vibes. *That's* music. That's the real thing!"

Performing with his band Earthworks.

here's a sort of a European percussionist aspect to my kit," says Bill Bruford of the evolution of his drum set, "whereby you let the composition dictate the kind of percussion you're going to use. Every tune you do, you kind of look at it afresh, and pretend first of all that you're not much of a drummer, and secondly that you don't have any instruments. Then you decide what would fit the music. The kit is a function of the composition that's being played.

"Sometimes it's the other way around. With Earthworks I had all these electronics and pads and I made percussive things as a way of offering a different backdrop for jazz players."

Bruford has consistently pushed the boundaries of the drum set, often redefining the drummer's role in the process. "Pretty much every gig you go to is going to have different parameters. Gone are the days when you just turn up with your drum kit. Bands have different colors to them and you try to enhance those with whatever you have available. This is where electronics come in. With King Crimson there is really noisy, dark metal stuff which I tend to trigger from pads and there is light, African slit drum things which can be played acoustically."

The drums have come a long way since the 1960s ,when Bruford first started playing. "My first drum kit cost 17 guinea, which was quite a lot then," he remembers. "It had a little thin red sparkle snare drum, really cheesy. Slowly I built up some serious drums. I got a set of Olympics, which were a sort of junior version of Premiers. It was red oyster pearl, which didn't look very hip, so I think I painted it black and put 'Ludwig' on the bass drum. In London in those days, Ludwig was what you needed to prove you were a real man. That was the first kit I had in Yes. Then one day the paint began to scrape off and I think they noticed I was kind of a fraud. I've felt a bit like a fraud ever since."

Bruford says his trademark snare drum sound, best heard on Yes songs like "Roundabout" and "Close to the Edge," was born out of necessity. "It started because it was a problem hearing the drums. There was no miking on the drums and the amplification was getting bigger and louder. I wasn't getting any cut, so I started to play rim shots all the time to get high frequencies out of the drum to penetrate the wall of sound from [Yes bassist] Chris Squire. I had a wide open drum with lots of overtones, which I still like. That became quite a difficult drum to record because the loud strokes were so loud and the light strokes so light. Engineers just wanted one dynamic. I began to be unpopular at studios. They would say, 'Why does that ringing have to be there, and why can't you play the center of the drum like the guy from Black Sabbath does?' I had a fairly weak left stick and it gave me more velocity and cut to use that particular sound. So the moral to that story I guess is we're all sort of a product of our disability."

Playing a mix-and-match kit of Ludwig and Hayman drums.

Bill onstage with King Crimson.

In the early 1980s, when most drummers were running away from the new electronic technology, Bruford embraced it with open arms. "There was this huge promise involving MIDI and drummers in the early eighties. Here was this new thing, drummers would be able to be anything at all. I'm a frustrated keyboard player anyway, so I'm inclined to play melodically. The idea that the drummer could play chords and pitches was very exciting to me. I got into it wholeheartedly, but it was very unreliable and hard to program. While it was clever and amazing what a drummer could do, there was a danger of it taking over the music. Just because the drummer could do it didn't mean it had to be used."

These days, with much more sensitive triggers and reliable samplers at his command, Bruford incorporates the technology as the music dictates. "Flexibility is everything. Suddenly as a drummer, you're able to adopt different roles, both melodically and abstractly. People say, 'Oh, electronics; it's a machine. You just push a button.' But it's very much flesh and blood."

In his role as rhythm pioneer, Bruford doesn't give much weight to rules. "I grew up with jazz and played jazz, then it became kind of a rock-jazz with Yes. But we had a classical keyboard player, Rick Wakeman, so all those rules went out the window. King Crimson is one of the last residual bands where you can adopt a strange approach. It's always been a stew and a mess, and that's the way I like it."

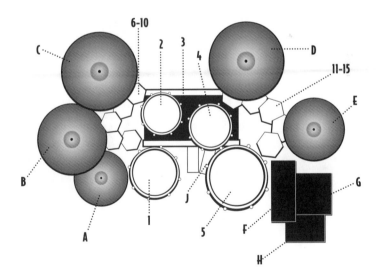

Bill Bruford's Kit 1994 ...Starclassic drums, Canary Yellow, w/Paiste cymbals

1... 6½ x 14" Snare Drum
2... 11 x 12" Tom-Tom
3... 22" Bass Drum
4... 12 x 13" Tom-Tom
5... 16 x 16" Floor Tom
6-15... Simmons SDX Pads

A... 14" Sound Edge Hi-hats
B... 18" Power Crash
C... 20" Flat Ride
D... 20" Dry Heavy Ride
E... 16" Power Crash
F... Yamaha DX II

G... Simmons SDX
H... Rack*
J... DW 5000 TE Electronic Bass
      Drum Pedal

*Alesis Quadraverb, Mapper, Emu Procussion, Simmons SPM 8.

Chad bearing the burden of the big beat.

Paul Beauchemin

Playing at the 1994 Modern Drummer Festival.

Don't get all serious trying to analyze the music of the Red Hot Chili Peppers with their drummer, Chad Smith; he's got his own view of the band. "We're like a giant exploding cosmic meatball that encompasses every orifice of your body," he says with mock self-importance. "That's on a good night. On a bad night, your shaking you're head, saying, 'What a bunch of clowns!'"

The Chilis serve up a bottom-heavy, booty-quaking hybrid of funk, hardcore, and rock all wrapped up in a big crazy package. Onstage, the band is half James Brown, half Sex Pistols, with Chad and bassist Flea at the eye of the storm, piloting a groove big enough to drive a truck through. "The Chili Peppers do everything, but it's really based in funk. To me, funk is party music. When we play live, it's all about having a party."

Growing up in Michigan in the seventies, Chad played drums in the high school marching band as well as local rock groups, all the while listening to drummers like Peter Criss, Mitch Mitchell, and John Bonham. "Bonham was the guy. His whole feel was just amazing. I owe my foot technique to just trying to emulate him. He was very musical and very funky. I love the way Mitch Mitchell just flowed over the kit. He really got my left hand into doing grace notes. Keith Moon made the drums seem like a really fun instrument. His personality came across in his drumming, which I think is important to having any kind of sound of your own."

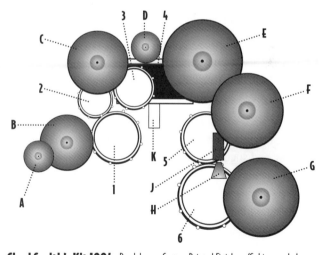

Chad Smith's Kit 1994...Pearl drums, Custom Painted Finish, w/Sabian cymbals

1... 7 x 14" Brady Snare Drum	C... 16" AA Medium Crash
2... 10 x 10" Tom-Tom	D... 8" AA Splash
3... 12 x 12" Tom-Tom	E... 21" AA Rock Ride
4... 22" Bass Drum	F... 19" AA Rock Crash
5... 14 x 14" Floor Tom	G... 20" AA Chinese
6... 16 x 16" Floor Tom	H... Cowbell
A... 8" CD Cymbal Disc	J... LP Jam Block
B... 14" AA Hi-hats	K... DW 5000 Bass Drum Pedal

Tom-Toms and cymbals mounted on a Pearl rack.
Special thanks to Louis Mathieu.

Jamming with brother Brad in the Smith basement, 1977.

After paying his dues in Midwestern bands like the Generics and Toby Redd, Chad moved out to Los Angeles to study drumming at PIT. On a friend's tip, he auditioned for the Peppers, joining the band for their breakthrough album, *Mothers Milk*, followed by the platinum-selling *Blood Sugar Sex Magik*.

"On *Blood Sugar* we had a lot of time before we recorded so we were really prepared. The songs didn't lend themselves to a lot of production; it was basically a job of being able to capture a good performance.

"The Peppers are a four-headed monster when it comes to the creative end. We don't have one songwriter; it's more about jamming and suggesting parts. A lot of songs just pop out of jams or spontaneous ideas. It's an equal thing and I really enjoy that freedom.

"Each song has its own space. Not every song should lay back; sometimes it should be aggressive. We spend a lot of time looking for the right feel. Certainly it's not about any fancy fills or anything technical. It's about trying to keep a good, exciting groove."

Chad plays Pearl drums and Sabian cymbals. One of his kits bears a fitting custom-painted scene of a whale and an octopus whose tentacles encompass the kit. "Ah, the underwater motif," notes Chad. "I'm into scuba diving, so that's where that comes from. The octopus and the whale are based on tattoos I have.

Maria [Chad's wife] sketched up some ideas and Johnny Douglas and Bill Detamore did the paint work. I had another painted kit that was stolen with all our equipment after a gig. Some kid's probably playing a bar mitzvah with it now.

"I've always liked the Pearl drums and stuck with them. It's kind of like an old shoe: you get used to how it feels, you're just comfortable with them. Same thing with Sabian. I'm a loyal guy; Sabian came along when I was a nobody and they were a new company. They gave me an endorsement. I was just so happy to get some cymbals that weren't broken.

"I'm paring down the drums. I think I'm gonna go the Bonham route—two crashes, a ride, and just bash. It'll make me play more straightforward. Less frills, no fills!"

On *Blood Sugar Sex Magik* Chad's drum sound was out in front of the mix, driving the beat home with conviction. "I like the drums to be organic, really natural and powerful sounding," he says. "I want it to sound like a live drum set, not like everything's been overdubbed. In the studio, I like to pick and choose with snare drums and cymbals, to get the right sound, see what fits the groove.

"It takes everybody to be in the pocket to make the drummer sound good. If you can see the guy in the back row bobbing his head, that's a really good feeling. Then I'm doing my job."

Kreutzmann and Hart with their arsenal of instruments.

Photo by the Author

Mickey Hart onstage at the Shoreline Amphitheater, 1994.

Photo by the Author

"We have never tried to explain our music," says Mickey Hart of the Grateful Dead "It's a more organic thing that happens at the moment. You like to think of it as great alchemy. It's music meant to alter consciousness; entertainment may be a by-product."

Hart is one half of a joined-at-the-drum duo of percussionists, the other half being Bill Kreutzmann. Together the two charm the rhythm beast for the Grateful Dead, providing a sonic feast of percussive sounds and noises. Onstage they have a huge array of drums, percussion, and electronics that they can access at any time. Kreutzmann's jazz-inflected drumming provides the foundation, while Hart's embellishes the beat. When listening to the two, the blend is so seamless, it's often hard to tell where one starts and the other leaves off. "We overlap a lot," says Kreutzmann, "which just evolved from years of playing together."

"I love the groove, but I love ornamentation as well," says Hart. "I like to come in and out of the groove and play with it, instead of living there all the time."

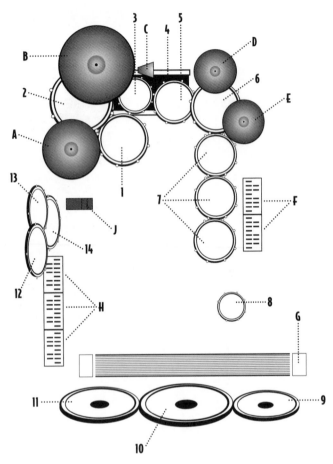

Mickey Hart's Kit 1994...Custom Shells and Finish drums w/Zildjian cymbals, Voelker Custom Rack

1... 8 x 14" Stave Snare Drum
2... 15 x 15" Tom-Tom
3... 8 x 10" Tom-Tom
4... 24" Bass Drum
5... 8 x 12" Tom-Tom
6... 14" Surdo
7... 3 Congas
8... Jaq Talking Drum
9... 20" Gong Drum
10... 28" Gong Drum
11... 24" Gong Drum
12... Falam

13... Timbale
14... Timbale
A... 15" Hi-hats
B... 20" Medium Ride
C... Cowbell
D... 12" Splash
E... 12" Splash
F... 2 Mallet KAT
G... The Beam
H... 3 Mallet KAT
J... Slit Drums

Special thanks to Ramrod.

Bill Kreutzmann's Kit 1994...Yamaha drums w/Zildjian cymbals

1... 6½ x 14" Noble & Cooley Snare Drum
2... 6 x 16" Octaban
3... 6 x 17" Octaban
4... 10 x 12" Tom-Tom
5... 11 x 13" Tom-Tom
6... 24" Bass Drum
7... 12 x 14" Tom-Tom
8... 16 x 16" Floor Tom
9... Jaq Talking Drum
10... LP Timbales

A... 15" Rock Hi-hats
B... 18" Medium Crash
C... 12" Splash
D... 22" Ping Ride
E... 8" Splash
F... 20" China
G... 10" Splash
H... 18" Crash
J... 4 Mallet KAT

Special thanks to Bill Grillo.

Kreutzmann and Hart's featured drum solo, which usually falls halfway into the second of two nightly sets, can be both jolting and sublime. In conjunction with the Dead's MIDI magician, Bob Bralove, the drummers mix acoustic and electronic sounds to create a tone picture that can literally shake the audience out of their seats. No two performances are alike. "I have any sound I want back there," explains Kreutzmann. "I'll tell Bob, our soundscape guy, the feelings I have on a certain night and what I want to get across, and he'll come up with the sounds to fit that feeling."

"We sample anything that sounds good," says Bralove. "Pots and pans, motorcycles, anything. Both guys trigger the sounds through Mallet KATs. I'm feeding a stereo image of that to the sound board."

"In drums," relates Hart, "if you want another sound, you have to get another drum. Luckily MIDI came along and allows us to take all those beautiful sounds from all those delicate instruments and travel and access those sounds over and over in many different ways. The advent of electronics has taken Billy and I from being trap drummers to becoming world percussionists. We've been fortunate enough to have one foot in the acoustic world and one foot in the amplified world. The dream for us is to deliver the payload to the audience, post haste."

Photo by the Author

Billy Kreutzmann behind the rack.

One of the most intriguing instruments available onstage is what is cryptically referred to as "The Beam." It has 13 strings stretched on a long piece of metal fitted with pickups. Hart coaxes and beats "The Beam" to get impressive and powerful sounds from it.

The two drummers have a full complement of acoustic drums; Kreutzmann plays a Yamaha kit with a Noble & Cooley snare drum, while Hart uses a custom set of drums assembled and painted by Gary Grimm from Eames shells. Hart keeps a 14"-diameter surdo drum and three congas on his right where a floor tom would traditionally go. "I put the surdo there because it's a different sound than the tom-toms," says Hart. "It isn't loud, but it has a reverberant sound."

Hart also keeps a Remo Falam, a type of high-pitched marching snare, on his left for special accents. "It's a real quick sound that stands out in a crowd," he says. "It wakes me up."

Kreutzmann has the lion's share of cymbals, while Hart uses his mostly for punctuation. "We had to simplify our cymbals," explains Kreutzmann, "because if each drummer uses a full complement, it's just way too much. Mostly the cymbals between us went away. I ride on my right side and Mickey rides on his left, so it separates it better sound-wise."

"We have enough cymbals in this band," says Hart. "Billy takes care of the crashes, so I'm playing the drums more."

When the Dead play, all six musicians in the band contribute to the groove, weaving in and out of syncopated rhythms, like a Dixieland band on acid. There is a free-form element to the music that keeps the players on their toes.

"Something should happen to you and you react right to it," explains Hart. "In order for the music to play you, you can't be in a rut; you must have constant surprises. You've got to be able to go out on the edge and not be afraid."

"I think about music as an experience, not as a technique," says Kreutzmann. "I hope the way I'm feeling is communicated to the audience. You just go out there and let the music take you away."

Dave onstage with Pearl Jam, 1994.

Lance Mercer

I don't play drums to make money," says Dave Abbruzzese, former skin slapper for Pearl Jam. "Being in a band is why I play drums. If there's ever a point where I listen to the music and I don't hear myself coming through it, it's time to move on to something else."

Abbruzzese is a hard-hitting, down-to-earth drummer, as straightforward a musician as you'll ever meet. In his playing he summons up power and finesse, using his strength to punch a groove into overdrive. Like so many young players, his drumming skills were honed over years of practicing in his room and playing in local bands. "One of my first gigs was at a place called Broadway Skateland when I was 12 or 13. It was so hilarious, two guitars in one amp, and the bass amp with bass and vocals. We got up there and I had these huge cymbals I had taken from the band room at school. The bass drum started to creep and one of the cymbals fell off the front of the stage and clocked this poor guy. Even with that, it was a great experience. The way I felt getting on my drums that day is the same way I feel when I play now. Nothing has changed.

Laying into his DW drums.

"I was heavy into Bonham when I was starting out; still am. I used to play along with all the records and memorize the parts. I love his sound. On *In through the Out Door* and *Presence*, those are real drums. Those Sly and the Family Stone records are great too. It just sounded like a dirty old funk kit, which is exactly what made those records happen. There's no sampling or triggers; it's just the real deal.

"Nothing personal to any drummers in the eighties, but the way a lot of records were produced, the drums did not sound like drums. They were reverbed and over-effected. It wasn't an acoustic set anymore. [Producer] Brendan O'Brien likes to work with the drums wide open. If you can get a real drum sound going, that's the best sound you can get.

"When I first started playing with Pearl Jam, my splash cymbals and all that freaked everybody out. It was too busy or just something they didn't want to hear as part of the music. After a while it became part of the music. I would still sneak things in to challenge myself. If you play a song 300 times, by the fiftieth time you're really ready to play it differently, even though you want to keep the integrity of the song."

Dave's cymbal technique and snare drum cracks are illustrated perfectly on "Go" and "Dissident" on Pearl Jam's second record, *Vs*. He likes to accent and heighten a song by using the many different cymbals on his kit. "I'm definitely a cymbal-heavy player," he explains. "I've got the [Sabian] AA14's and AAX 14" China. They both have the same texture but two totally different bites. I love China cymbals. Splashes are great, because to me, nothing is more textural.

"I was playing my Ludwig kit when I first joined Pearl Jam. It was really big Bonham drums, and I drove our sound man crazy. While we were in Europe, John Good from DW brought out a set for me to try. It had a 22" bass and 12, 16, and 18" toms. I loved the kit. Then I started hearing all these smaller toms that actually sounded bigger. When we went into the studio, I got a 10, 12, 14, and 16" tom kit and it was really happening. I was playing a Brady 12" snare and liked it, so I had DW make the 12 x 7" for me."

When Pearl Jam played the big venues Dave found a way to personalize his performance and keep his mind on why he played the drums. "I remember what it was like going to see my favorite bands. If I get up on my kit and in the first five seconds I see somebody looking at me, then it's their show. They are the ones I'm doing it for."

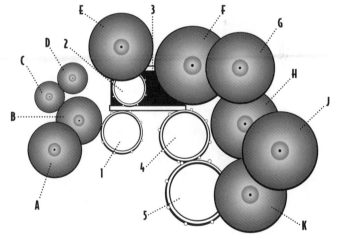

Dave Abbruzzese's Kit 1994...DW drums, White Finish, w/Sabian cymbals

1... 7 x 12" Snare Drum		**D**... 8" AA Splash	
2... 9 x 10" Tom-Tom		**E**... 17" AAX Stage Crash	
3... 22" Bass Drum		**F**... 20" AAX Metal Ride	
4... 12 x 14" Floor Tom		**G**... 18" AAX Stage Crash	
5... 14 x 16" Floor Tom		**H**... 18" AA Fast Chinese	
A... 14" AAX Metal Chinese		**J**... 20" AA Chinese	
B... 13" AAX Fusion Hi-hats		**K**... 19" AA Medium Thin Crash	
C... 8" AAX Splash			

Adrift on a sea of drums, 1994.

Andrew MacNaughton

When you buy a ticket to a Rush concert, you know that you are going to get your money's worth. It's always an entertaining evening of rock spectacle. Bassist and vocalist Geddy Lee and guitarist Alex Lifeson deliver the goods, playing compositions culled from over 20 years of material. But for many people a Rush show is like a trip to drum heaven, made complete by the presence of Neil Peart's elegantly artful drumming. Peart has made an occupation of making the inconceivable happen on the drum kit. He has also influenced a generation of drummers to take risks and fear no musical challenge.

One of the most interesting aspects of Neil's career with Rush is the evolution of his drum set. When the band started touring in the 1970s, Neil had a fairly big outfit to complement the music that was being played. Through the eighties and into the nineties, his setup has changed dramatically to accommodate the needs of the music. The advent of electronics and digital sampling have added a whole new dimension of sound to his already sizable palette.

Working hard onstage with Rush, 1994.

A Rush tour is a serious undertaking, considering the logistics involved. A great amount of equipment needs to be transported, set up, played, and broken down every day. Larry Allen, Peart's longtime drum tech, has the responsibility for making it all run smoothly. When you see the size of Peart's kit, it's not surprising it takes Allen a good amount of time to assemble, clean, and maintain the drums, cymbals, hardware, and electronics. Both Allen and Peart take great pride in planning for every contingency on the road, making sure that all runs smoothly for the evening's show. "It's a very special thing to me to make sure that drum kit is 100% perfect for Neil to come up and play," says Allen.

The drum set itself (actually two complete kits, one acoustic and one electronic) is a behemoth: 13 acoustic drums, 15 cymbals, 8 trigger pads, one MIDI mallet controller, and various bells, pedals, and accessories. The drums are not for show; Peart has a use for every piece of equipment onstage.

Central to the acoustic kit is a 1960s vintage 5 x 14" Slingerland Artists Model snare drum that Peart has used for many years. "My favorite 'working' drum is still my old Slingerland," he told *Modern Drummer*'s William Miller. "I've had it for years and it's never let me down...That drum is a wonder—it's sensitive and aggressive." "That is *the* drum," says Allen. "It sounds fabulous."

The Ludwigs Peart uses are given a thin inside coat of a substance called Vibrafibe, by Larry Allen's company XL Specialty Percussion. Allen says this promotes better sound projection of the shells. For his electronic setup, Neil triggers sounds from four Akai S900 samplers through the various pads on the kit. All the drum and cymbal stands on the rotating drum riser are attached by screwing specially made mounts into the base of the drum boards.

As complicated as the setup sounds, it doesn't seem to matter once Peart takes the stage. The seamless fills and intricate beats appear to come naturally to him as he takes the art of drumming into the upper stratosphere.

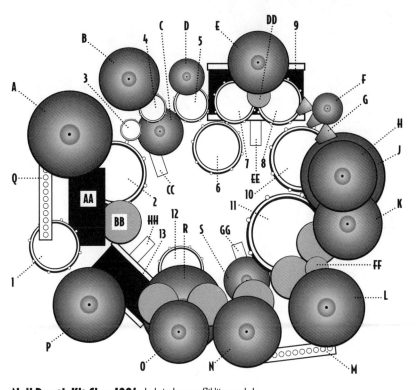

Neil Peart's Kit Circa 1994...Ludwig drums w/Zildjian cymbals

1... 3 x 14" Remo Legato Snare Drum	**A**... 20" Crash	**O**... 16" Crash
2... 16 x 16" Floor Tom	**B**... 16" Crash	**P**... 19" Wuhan China
3... 5½ x 6" Double-Headed Tom	**C**... 13" New Beat Hi-hats	**Q**... Wind Chimes
4... 5½ x 8" Double-Headed Tom	**D**... 10" Splash	**R**... 22" Ride
5... 8 x 10" Tom-Tom	**E**... 16" Crash	**S**... 13" New Beat Hi-hats
6... 5 x 14" Slingerland Snare Drum	**F**... 8" Splash	**AA**... Mallet KAT
7... 8 x 12" Tom-Tom	**G**... 1 Small Cowbell, Triple Agogo Bells, 1 Large Cowbell	**BB**... 6 D Drum Pads
8... 9 x 13" Tom-Tom	**H**... 18" Crash	**CC**... Shark Pedals
9... 24" Bass Drum	**J**... 22" Ride	**DD**... SID Electronic Trigger
10... 13 x 15" Floor Tom	**K**... 18¾" Wuhan China	**EE**... Yamaha Double Bass Drum Pedal
11... 22" Gong Bass Drum, 24" Head	**L**... 20" Swish	**FF**... Dauz Pad Keyboard Trigger
12... 3 x 13" Ensemble Snare Drum	**M**...Wind Chimes	**GG**... Shark Pedals
13... 18" Bass Drum	**N**... 18" Crash	**HH**...Camco Bass Drum Pedal

Special thanks to Larry Allen and *Modern Drummer*.

The peerless Mr. Williams.

Photo by Vernon Vega

As far as the art of drumming can go, you can be sure Tony Williams will take it there, making real the impossible and doing it with confidence and flair. His additional talents as a composer and bandleader only serve to enhance his reputation as a musical renaissance man.

You don't get hired into Miles Davis' band at age 17 if you don't show a tremendous amount of promise. Davis recruited Williams because he was blown away by Tony's ability and style. Williams became part of a great quintet that included Davis, Herbie Hancock, Wayne Shorter, and Ron Carter. "There ain't but one Tony Williams when it comes to playing the drums," wrote Miles. "There was nobody like him before or since."

With Ron Carter and his yellow Gretsch kit, 1980s.

After an association that spanned most of the 1960s, Tony left Miles and formed Lifetime, a raw mix of jazz and rock that included fellow Davis alumnus John McLaughlin on guitar. Lifetime was one of the prototypical fusion bands of the late sixties and seventies. As he had done with the Davis quintet, Williams created a new vocabulary of drumming that transcended traditional approaches.

After two versions of Lifetime and some solo records, Williams eventually formed a quintet in the mid eightie's to showcase his ever-growing library of compositions. The band was one of the finest groups in the business, critically acclaimed and artistically successful.

"I'm really just interested in a good sound," he told *Modern Drummer.* "I tune [the drums] so they'll sound good together in a group." "My love for the instrument caused me to want to play it beautifully," he remarked to another interviewer.

Williams plays Zildjian cymbals and switched to DW drums after being identified with his yellow Gretsch kit for so many years. His wide open sound results from a combination of thoughtful tuning, Remo CS clear batter heads, and the powerful stroke he has developed. "I like to place my drums and cymbals a fair distance away from me so that I can get a good healthy swing," he told writer Aran Wald. "I really believe in sitting and having my hands in a balanced position."

His dazzling solos are without equal, combining fearless speed and independence with masterful technique and musicality, building layers of sound with his drums and cymbals. Williams celebrates the power of the drum set, using dynamics and textures to paint a canvas of tone and accent. When introducing the members of his band, it is not unusual for Williams to point out his kit as an equal participant in the music. "These drums have taken me around the world," he says with the pride and respect a great artist has for his tools.

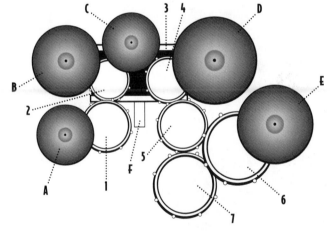

Tony Williams' Kit 1994...DW drums, Solid Yellow Finish, w/Zildjian cymbals

1... 6½ x 14" Solid Maple Shell Snare Drum
2... 9 x 12" Tom-Tom
3... 24" Bass Drum
4... 10 x 13" Tom-Tom
5... 14 x 14" Floor Tom
6... 14 x 18" Floor Tom
7... 14 x 16" Floor Tom

A... 15" K Hi-hats
B... 18" K Dark Crash Medium Thin
C... 15" K Dark Crash Thin
D... 22" K Ride
E... 20" K Dark Crash
F... DW 5000 Turbo Bass Drum Pedal

All lugs and hoops are finished in a red powder coating. The stands are powder coated in a black finish. Remo clear BlackDot CS heads are used on all drums. Tony also owns a small bebop kit and a double bass drum rock kit.

An early incarnation of Billy's Fibes kit.

Billy with his massive kit in London, mid 1970s.

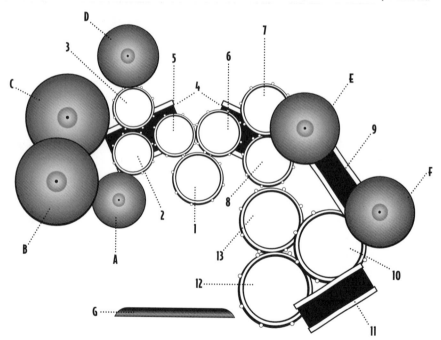

Billy Cobham's Kit Circa 1976...Fibes drums, Clear Fiberglass, North Tom-Tom, Al Duffy & Jeff Ochletree Custom-Made Snare & Gong drums, w/Zildjian cymbals

1... 7 x 14" Al Duffy Custom Snare Drum	**8**... 14 x 14" Tom-Tom	**B**... 22" Swish
2... 8 x 12" Tom-Tom	**9**... 22" Gong Drum	**C**... 22" Ride
3... 12" North Tom-Tom	**10**...18 x 18" Floor Tom	**D**... 16" Crash
4... 2 - 24" Bass Drums	**11**... 24" Gong Drum	**E**... 18" Crash
5... 8 x 12" Tom-Tom	**12**...20 x 20" Floor Tom	**F**... 18" Crash
6... 9 x 13" Tom-Tom	**13**...16 x 16" Floor Tom	**G**... 36" Gong
7... 14" North Tom-Tom	**A**... 14" Hi-hats*	

*Hi-hats attached to bass drum.

Photo by the Author

Framed by his Starclassic kit.

Photo by the Author

Simon playing at the Modern Drummer Festival, 1994.

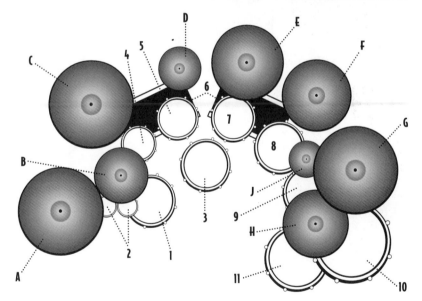

Simon Phillips' Kit Circa 1994...Starclassic drums, Ruby Red Maple, w/Zildjian cymbals

1... 3¼ x 14" Snare Drum
2... 4 - Octabans
3... 6½ x 14" Snare Drum
4... 9 x 10" Tom-Tom
5... 10 x 12" Tom-Tom
6... 2 - 24" Bass Drums
7... 11 x 13" Tom-Tom

8... 12 x 14" Tom-Tom
9... 14 x 15" Floor Tom
10... 14 x 20" Gong Drum
11... 15 x 16" Floor Tom
A... 22" A Custom Swish
B... 14" A Custom Hi-hats
C... 22" A Custom Ride

D... 12" K Splash Brilliant
E... 19" A Custom Crash
F... 18" A Custom Crash
G... 22" A China
H... 17" A Custom Crash
J... 10" A Special Recording Hats

Thanks to Joe Hibbs.

With his custom Pork Pie drums.

Tim playing his huge array of percussion, 1994.

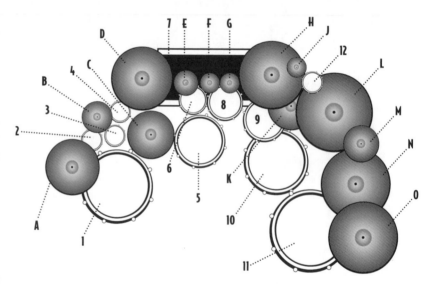

Tim Alexander's Kit 1994...Pork Pie drums w/Zildjian cymbals

1... 14 x 18" Gong Bass
2... 30 x 6" Clear Tube Drum
3... 15 x 6" Clear Tube Drum
4... 20 x 6" Clear Tube Drum
5... 5½ x 14" Ludwig Snare Drum
6... 8 x 8" Tom-Tom
7... 20" Bass Drum
8... 9 x 10" Tom-Tom
9... 10 x 12" Tom-Tom

10... 14 x 16" Floor Tom
11... 18 x 22" Large Tom
12... 25 x 6" Clear Tube Drum
A... 14" China
B... 8" EFX
C... 13" Hi-hats*
D... 16" K Crash
E... 6" EFX
F... 4" Splash

G... 4" Brilliant Splash
H... 17" Rock Crash
J... LP Ice Bell
K... 13" Hi-hats*
L... 20" Impulse Ride
M... 10" Chow Gong
N... 18" Wuhan China
O... 18" Rock Crash

*Hi-hats are Dynobeat top with New Beat bottom.
Note: Hardware is Yamaha with Gibraltar rack system, Roc-N-Soc throne, and Tama strapdrive bass drum pedals.

Special thanks to **Modern Drummer**.

Courtesy Zildjian Co.

In the studio with Yes, 1970s.

Photo by the Author

Sound check with Yes, 1994 tour.

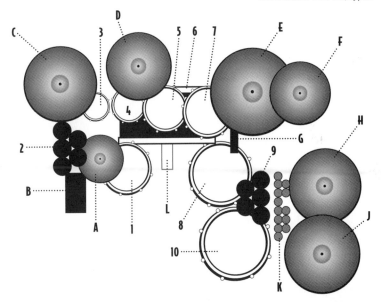

Alan White's Kit 1994...Ludwig drums, Custom Red Sparkle Finish, RIMS Mounts and Collarlock Rack w/Zildjian cymbals

1... 6½ x 14" Bronze Snare Drum	**8**... 16 x 16" Tom-Tom	**E**... 22" Custom Ping
2... ddrum Pads	**9**... ddrum Pads	**F**... 16" A Custom
3... 8 x 8" Tom-Tom	**10**...16 x 18" Tom-Tom	**G**... Reek Havoc Trigger Pad
4... 8 x 10" Tom-Tom	**A**... 13" A Custom Hi-hats	**H**... 19" K China
5... 12 x 13" Tom-Tom	**B**... Drum KAT	**J**... 20" A China Boy Low
6... 24" Bass Drum	**C**... 19" A Custom Crash	**K**... Crotales
7... 13 x 14" Tom-Tom	**D**... 17" A Custom Crash	**L**... Axis Double Bass Drum Pedal

Rack hardware includes: E-mu Procussion, Proteus 2+3, Dynacord MIDI controller, and E-mu E3XP Turbo Emulator sampler.
Note: Alan uses Remo Ambassador heads and Axis trigger pedals (not shown). There is a subwoofer mounted to the bottom of his throne to augment the earplug monitors he wears.
Thanks to Jim Robison.

BIBLIOGRAPHY

Aldridge, John. *Guide to Vintage Drums*. Fullerton, CA: Centerstream Publishing, 1994.

Balliett, Whitney. *American Musicians: 56 Portraits in Jazz*. New York: Oxford University Press, 1986.

———. *Goodbyes and Other Messages: A Journal of Jazz, 1981–1990*. New York: Oxford University Press, 1991.

Basie, Count, with Murray, Albert. *Good Morning Blues: The Autobiography of Count Basie*. New York: Random House, 1985.

Blaine, Hal, with Goggin, David. *Hal Blaine and the Wrecking Crew*. Emeryville, CA: Mix Books, 1990.

Cook, Rob. *The Complete History of the Leedy Drum Company*. Fullerton, CA: Centerstream Publishing, 1993.

Crowther, Bruce. *Gene Krupa: His Life & Times*. New York: Universe Books, 1987.

Davis, Miles, with Troupe, Quincy. *Miles: The Autobiography*. New York: Simon & Schuster, 1989.

Davis, Stephen. *Hammer of the Gods: The Led Zeppelin Saga*. New York: Ballantine Books, 1985.

Dodds, Baby, with Gara, Larry. *The Baby Dodds Story*. Baton Rouge: Louisiana State University Press, 1992.

Enstice, Wayne, and Rubin, Paul. *Jazz Spoken Here: Conversations With 22...Musicians*. Baton Rouge: Louisiana State University Press, 1992.

Escort, Colin, with Hawkins, Martin. *Good Rockin' Tonight: Sun Records and the Birth of Rock and Roll*. New York: St. Martin's Press, 1991.

Gillespie, Dizzy, with Fraser, Al. *To Be, or Not...To Bop: Memoirs*. New York: Doubleday & Co., 1979.

Hart, Mickey, and Lieberman, Frederic. *Planet Drum*. San Francisco: Harper, 1991.

Korall, Burt. *Drummin' Men*. New York: Macmillan Co., 1990.

Lewisohn, Mark. *The Beatles Day by Day: A Chronology 1962–1989*. New York: Harmony Books, 1987.

———. *The Complete Beatles Chronicle*. New York: Harmony Books, 1992.

Licks, Dr. [Alan Slutsky]. *Standing in the Shadows of Motown: The Life and Music of Legendary Bassist James Jamerson*. Wynnewood, PA: Dr. Licks Publishing, 1989.

Mitchell, Mitch, with Platt, John. *Jimi Hendrix: Inside the Experience*. New York: St. Martin's Press, 1990.

Murray, Charles Shaar. *Crosstown Traffic: Jimi Hendrix and the Rock and Roll Revolution*. New York: St. Martin's Press, 1989.

Pinksterboer, Hugo. *The Cymbal Book*. Edited by Rick Mattingly. Milwaukee: Hal Leonard, 1992.

Rosenthal, David H. *Hard Bop: Jazz and Black Music 1955–1965*. New York: Oxford University Press, 1992.

Schmidt, Paul William. *History of the Ludwig Drum Company*. Fullerton, CA: Centerstream Publishing, 1991.

Schuller, Gunther. *The Swing Era: The Development of Jazz 1930–1945*. New York: Oxford University Press, 1989.

Simon, George. *The Big Bands*. New York: Macmillan Co., 1974.

Tormé, Mel. *Traps: The Drum Wonder*. New York: Oxford University Press, 1991.

Weinberg, Max, with Santelli, Robert. *The Big Beat*. Chicago: Contemporary Books, 1984.

Wexler, Jerry, and Ritz, David. *Rhythm and the Blues: A Life in American Music*. New York: Alfred A. Knopf, 1993.

Magazine sources: *DRUM!*
 Drums and Drumming
 Modern Drummer
 Rhythm